UTOPIA

HOLME MILLS, BURTON IN KENDAL,
CARNFORTH, LANCS

Tel: (0524) 781 · 739

The Price Guide to
Pine Furniture
and
Kitchenalia

Compiled & Edited by

Judith & Martin Miller

Assistant Editor
Elizabeth Smith

A Miller's Guide

MJM Publications

ANN LINGARD

ROPE WALK ANTIQUES
RYE, SUSSEX
TEL: (0797) 223486
(difficult to find)

Directions: Off Cinque Port Street opposite
Conduit Street

5,000 square feet of well finished
**PINE FURNITURE
KITCHENALIA ANTIQUES
DECORATIVE OBJECTS**

*Monday–Saturday 10.00–5.30
Sunday by Appointment*

Contents

Copyright © MJM Publications Ltd.
Printed and Bound in Great Britain
by William Clowes Ltd.,
Beccles and London
Published by MJM Publications Ltd.
The Grange, Benenden, Cranbrook,
Kent TN17 4DN
Telephone: Cranbrook (0580) 240454
Designers Groom and Pickerill
Original Photography by Mel Lewis
40 Lordship Rd. London N16 0QT

6

Key to Illustrations

AA   Anvil Antiques, Old Step Row & The Old School, Alsop Street, Leek, Staffs. Tel: (0538) 371657

Ad   Adams Antiques, 47 Chalk Farm Road, N.W.1. Tel: 01.267 9241

AH   Abbotts House Antiques, 25 White Hart Street, Aylsham, Norfolk. Tel: (026 373) 4182

AL   Ann Lingard, Rope Walk Antiques, Rye, Sussex. Tel: (0797) 223486

APP   Antique Pine Partners, 18 Courcy Road, N.8. Tel: 01.739 7423

BA   T. Bannister & Co., Market Place, Haywards Heath, W. Sussex. Tel: (0444) 412402

Bed   Bed of Roses Antiques, 12 Prestbury Road, Cheltenham, Glos. Tel: (0242) 31918

BEL   Bell Antiques, 68 Harold Street, Grimsby, S. Humberside. Tel: (0472) 695110

BHW   Butler & Hatch Waterman, High Street, Tenterden, Kent. Tel: (05 806) 3233 (Also at High Street, Hythe, Kent.)

C   Christie, Manson & Woods Ltd., 8 King Street, S.W.1 Tel: 01.839 9060

CDC   Capes, Dunn & Co., The Auction Galleries, 38 Charles Street, Manchester, Lancs. Tel: (061 273) 6060

CGC   Cheffins, Grain & Chalk, 49-53 Regent Street, Cambridge. Tel: (0223) 58721/6

Ch   Chancery Antiques, 8/10 Barrington Street, Tiverton, Devon. Tel: (0884) 252416

Co   Country Antiques, Castle Mill, Kidwelly, Dyfed. Tel: (0554) 890534

COR   Corinium Antiques, 23 Gloucester Street, Cirencester, Glos. Tel: (0285) 2839

CRA   The Craftsman, 16 Bridge Street, Hungerford, Berks. Tel: (0488) 82262

CRP   Chris Roper's Pine Shop, 312 Welford Road, Leicester. Tel: 0533 704553

D   Domus, Woodcock Street, Castle Cary, Somerset. Tel: (0963) 50912

Del   Delta Antiques, 175-177 Smithdown Road, Liverpool, Merseyside. Tel: (051 734) 4277

DH   Daniels House Antiques, Hoggs Hill Street, Beaminster, Devon. Tel: (0308) 862635

DPN   David & Penny Newlove Antiques, 28 High Street, Wincanton, Somerset. Tel: (0963) 32672

DT   Dickenson & Thomas, The Old Granary, 10 North Street, Stamford, Lincs. Tel: (0780) 62236

En   Enloc Antiques, Old Corporation Yard, Knotts Lane, Colne, Lancs. Tel: (0282) 861417

Far   The Farmhouse, The Fourth Avenue, The Covered Market, Oxford. Tel: (0865) 247084

FA   Fagins Antiques, 28/29 Albion Street, Exmouth, Devon. Tel: (0395) 266602

FRM   Frank R. Marshall & Co., Chelford Agricultural Centre, Chelford, Cheshire. Tel: (0625) 861122

GF   Genges Farm Antiques, Genges Farm, Limington, Nr. Yeovil, Somerset. Tel: (0935) 840464

GHM   Gerry Haddock's Hand Made Furniture, The Covered Yard, King Street, Lancaster. Tel: (0524) 63404

GLF   Green Lane Farm, Bethersden, Kent. Tel: (023 382) 382

HD   Halcyon Days, 14 Brook Street, W.1. Tel: 01.629 8811

HG   Hay Galleries, 4 High Town, Hay Town, Hay-on-wye, Hereford. Tel: (0497) 820356

HH   Herald House Antiques, North Street, Langport, Somerset. Tel: (0458) 250587

Hil   Hillside Antiques, Balcombe Road, Pound hill, Crawley, Sussex. Tel: (0293) 883379/884018

MB   Manor Barn Pine, Burnside Mill, Main Street, Addingham, Ilkley, W. Yorks. Tel: (0943) 830176

MPA   Market Place Antiques, 35 Market Place, Henley-on-Thames, Oxon. Tel: (049 12) 2387

MV   Milverton Antiques, Fore Street, Milverton, Taunton, Somerset. Tel: (0823) 400597

OC   Olwen Carthew, 109 Kirkdale, S.E.26. Tel: 01.699 1353

OPS   Old Pine Shop, 27 Gloucester Road, Ross-on-Wye, Herefordshire. Tel: (0989) 64738

OR   The Old Rectory Country Furniture, The Old Rectory, Loxley, Stratford-upon-Avon, Warwicks. Tel: (0789) 840254

PC   Private Collection

PCA   Pine & Country Antiques, Sandhill Barn, Washington, W. Sussex. Tel: (0903) 892888

PCo   The Pine Company, 104 Christchurch Road, Ringwood, Hants. Tel: (04254) 3932

PF   Pine Finds, The Old Cornmill, Bishop Monkton, Harrogate, N. Yorks. Tel: (0765) 87159

PH   M. Deardon, Pennard House, East Pennard, Shepton Mallet, Somerset. Tel: (074 986) 266

PJ   Peter James Antiques, 168-170 Devonshire Street, Sheffield 3, S. Yorks. Tel: (0742) 700273

RAB   R. A. Berry Antiques, Manor Farm, Cotham, Newark, Notts. Tel: (0636) 71728

RB   Robert Barley Antiques, 48 Fulham High Street, S.W.6. Tel: 01.736 4429

RC   Ray Coggins Antiques, The Old Brewery, Newtown, Bradford-on-Avon, Wilts. Tel: (022 16) 3431

RK   Richard Kimbell, Harborough Road, Desborough, Nr. Kettering, Northants. Tel: (0536) 762041

S   Sotheby, Parke Bernet & Co., 34-35 New Bond Street, W.1. Tel: 01.493 8080

SC   Sotheby's, Chester, Booth Mansion, Watergate Street, Chester, Cheshire. Tel: (0244) 315531

SAL   Shamrock Antiques Limited, Killanley, Ballina, Co. Mayo, Ireland. Tel: (096) 36275

Sca   Scallywag, The Old Church, Wren Road, Camberwell Green, S.E.5 Tel: 01.701 5353

ST   Scar Top Antiques, Far Scar Top, Stanbury, Keighley, W. Yorks. Tel: (0535) 42585

SW   Stone-Wares, The Stripped Pine Shop, 24 Radford Street, Stone, Staffs. Tel: (0785) 815000

UP   Utopia Pine, Holme Mills, Carnforth, Lancs. Tel: (0524) 781739

VI   Victorian Interiors, 12 Boundary Road, Hove, Sussex. Tel: (0273) 423384

W   Woodstock, 1563/1565 London Road, Norbury, S.W.16. Tel: 01.764 0270 (Also at Furniture Cave, 533 King's Road, S.W.3. Tel: 01.352 2046)

WH   Wych House Antiques, Wych Hill, Woking, Surrey. Tel: (048 62) 64635

YP   Yesterday's Pine, The Mill, Beehive Street, Retford, Notts. Tel: (0777) 706256

YSS   Antique Pine, Yorkshire Stripping Service, Mill Farm, Kirk Hammerton, Yorks. Tel: (0901) 30451

Some entries in this Guide have been left without a code. These have been drawn from Miller's 'photo library and an up-to-date valuation has been given.

Jos   Jose Hornsey, 3 Silver Street, Bradford-on-Avon, Wilts. Tel: (022 16) 4333

LRG   Lots Road Galleries, 71 Lots Road, Chelsea, N.W.10 Tel: 01.352 234

9

Here we have, probably the largest country pine showroom in the British Isles, with a staggering stock of beautifully restored antique pieces that really make your mouth water. Also a comprehensive variety of reproduction pine to compliment the old, enabling you to furnish your entire home from one source.

With quality that is of the highest order and prices that are so hard to beat, you soon realise after entering this Aladdin's Cave of pine why it has become such a popular hunting ground for pine enthusiasts.

From the smallest box to a glazed bookcase that is fully 15 feet long the antique pine has been brought from all corners of the U.K. and Europe.

A complete range of English country chairs heads a variety of reproduction furniture designed to replace the old, no longer or rarely obtainable and gives us pieces that were never made but are much needed in the 1980's.

Built entirely on reputation and hard work over a period of 13 years, and refusing to let standards of service drop, Scallywag is surely a place that must be visited by all.

11

Directory of Specialists

London

Adams Antiques,
47 Chalk Farm Road, N.W.1.
Tel: 01.267 9241

Antique Pine Partners,
18 Courcy Road, N.8.
Tel: 01.739 7423

C. W. Buckingham,
301-303 Munster Road, S.W.6.
Tel: 01.385 2657

Furniture Cave,
533 Kings Road, S.W.6.
Tel: 01.352 2046

Guinevere Antiques,
578/580 Kings Road, S.W.6.
Tel: 01.736 2917

Nicholas Beech Antiques,
787 Wandsworth Road, S.W.8.
Tel: 01.720 8552

Olwen Carthew,
109 Kirkdale, S.E. 26.
Tel: 01.699 1363

Princedale Antiques,
56 Eden Grove, N.7
Tel: 01.727 0868

Savile Pine,
560 Kings Road, S.W.6
Tel: 01.736 3625

Scallywag,
The Old Church,
Wren Road, Camberwell Green,
S.E.5.
Tel: 01.701 5353

The Pine Mine,
96-100 Wandsworth Bridge Road,
S.W. 6.
Tel: 01.736 1092

The Village Workshop,
19 Chalk Farm Road, N.W.1
Tel: 01.482 2319

This & That,
50-51 Chalk Farm Road,
N.W.1 8AN
Tel: 01.267 5433

Wimbledon Pine Co.,
246 Haydons Road,
Wimbledon, S.W.19.
Tel: 01.540 5032

Wooden Heart
55 New Kings Road, S.W.6.
Tel: 01.731 5931

Woodstock, 1563/1565 London Road,
Norbury, S.W.16.
Tel: 01.764 0270

Avon

Abbas Combe Pine,
4 Upper Maudlin Street, Bristol.
Tel: (0272) 299023

Widcombe Antiques & Pine,
9 Claverton Buildings, Widcombe,
Bath.
Tel: (0225) 28767

Beds.

Ampthill Antiques Centre,
Market Square, Ampthill.
Tel: (0525) 403344

Ann Roberts Antiques
Kings Arms Yard, Ampthill.
Tel: (0525) 403394

Hagen Restorations,
Bakehouse Cottage, Haynes.
Tel: (023 066) 424

S. & S. Timms Antiques Ltd.,
18 Dunstable Street, Ampthill.
Tel: (0525) 403067

Timms Antiques, 23 Church Square,
Toddington.
Tel: (052 55) 2259

Yesterday's Pine,
13 Dunstable Street, Ampthill.
Tel: (0525) 402260

Berks.

Jurich Properties Ltd.,
28 Beaumont Road, Windsor.
Tel: (075 35) 51548

The Craftsman, 16 Bridge Street,
Hungerford.
Tel: (0488) 82262

Bucks.

Flames, Hill Avenue,
Amersham-on-the-Hill.
Tel: (024 03) 7410

For Pine,
4 Broad Street, Chesham.
Tel: (0494) 776119

Interpine,
High Street, Stony Stratford.
Tel: (0908) 568004

Peter Jones Antiques,
10 Market Place, Chalfont
St. Peter.
Tel: (0753) 883367

Liz Quilter,
38 High Street, Amersham.
Tel: (024 03) 3723

Market Place Antiques,
Market Place, Olney.
Tel: (0234) 712172

The Pine Merchants,
52 High Street, Great Missenden.
Tel: (024 06) 2002

Cambs

Acorn,
12 Lensfield Road, Cambridge.
Tel: (0223) 357636

Audraw Limited,
High Street, Soham.
Tel: (0353) 720342

Doddington House Antiques,
2 Benwick Road, Doddington.
Tel: (0354) 740755

Dudley's Antiques & Home Interiors,
Vine House, Fair Green, Reach.
Tel: (0638) 741989

Langhorn Antiques,
Langhorn Lane, Outwell.
Tel: (0945) 772668

Mere Antiques,
High Street, Fowlmere.
Tel: (076 382) 477

Paul Micklin Antiques,
1 & 3 Church Street, Whittlesey.
Tel: (0733) 204355

Riro D. Mooney,
4 Moorfield Road, Duxford.
Tel: (0223) 832252

The Golden Drop Antiques,
Chatteris Road, Warboys.
Tel: (035 43) 2990

The Pine Cone,
15 Gwydir Street, Cambridge.
Tel: (0223) 311203

West Farm Antiques,
High Street, Orwell.
Tel: (0223) 207464

Cheshire

Richmond Galleries,
1st Floor, Watergate Buildings,
New Crane Street, Chester.
Tel: (0244) 317602

Stewart Evans,
Church Street, Malpas.
Tel: (0948) 860214

Co. Durham

Horsemarket Antiques,
27 Horsemarket, Barnard Castle.
Tel: (0833) 37881

Cornwall

Lamborne Manor Antiques,
Radnor, Nr. Redruth.
Tel: (0209) 890218

Derbyshire

Antique Coffee House,
Buxton Road, Bakewell.
Tel: (062 981) 3544

Bygones,
230 Derby Road, Heanor.
Tel: (0773) 768503

Melbourne Treasure Chest,
58 Potter Street, Melbourne.
Tel: (033 16) 3399

Old Farmhouse Furniture,
Parwick Lees Farm, Ashbourne.
Tel: (0335) 25473

Old Pine,
1 Millford Road, Duffield.
Tel: (0332) 841146

Spurrier Smith,
23B Church Street, Ashbourne.
Tel: (0335) 43669

The Sweetings,
1a The Buffs, Alfreton.
Tel: (0773) 825930

Wooden Box Antiques,
32 High Street, Woodville,
Burton-on-Trent.
Tel: (0283) 212014

Devon

Chancery Antiques,
8/10 Barrington Street, Tiverton.
Tel: (0884) 252416/253190

Drawers,
45 Plymouth Road, Buckfastleigh.
Tel: (0364) 42848

Fagins Antiques,
28/29 Albion Street, Exmouth.
Tel: (0395) 266602

Fine Pine of Harbertonford,
Woodland Road, Harbertonford.
Tel: (080 423) 465

Waterwheel Pine & Antiques,
Cricklepit Mill, The Quay, Exeter.
Tel: (0392) 217076

A. T. Whitton,
151 Fore Street, Exeter.
Tel: (0392) 73377

Dorset

Country Pine Antiques,
The Green, Sherborne.
Tel: (0935) 815216

Daniels House Antiques,
Hogshill Street, Beaminster.
Tel: (0308) 862635

David Lane Antiques,
The Old Forge,
Compton Abbas, Shaftesbury.
Tel: (0747) 811881

Essex

Southend Pine,
468-470a Southchurch Road,
Southend.
Tel: (0702) 64649

Glos.

Bed of Roses Antiques,
12 Prestbury Road, Cheltenham.
Tel: (0242) 31918

Corinium Antiques,
23 Gloucester Street, Cirencester.
Tel: (0285) 2839

Gloucester House Antiques,
Market Place, Fairford.
Tel: (0285) 3066

Wye Antiques,
The Square, Stow-on-the-Wold.
Tel: (0451) 31004

Hants.

C. W. Buckingham,
Twin Firs, Southampton Road,
Cadnam.
Tel: (0703) 812122

Phoenix House Antiques,
Old Corner Shop, Phoenix Green,
Hartley Wintney, Basingstoke.
Tel: (025 126) 4430

The Pine Cellars,
38 Jewry Street, Winchester.
Tel: (0962) 67014

The Pine Company,
104 Christchurch Road,
Ringwood.
Tel: (042 54) 3932

Hereford

Hay Galleries Limited,
4 High Town, Hay-on-Wye.
Tel: (0497) 820356

La Barre Limited,
The Place, 116 South Street,
Leominster.
Tel: (0568) 4315

Old Pine Shop,
Gloucester Road, Ross-on-Wye.
Tel: (0989) 64738

Herts.

M. & S. Armson,
370 High Street, Berkhamsted.
Tel: (044 27) 2241

Careless Cottage Antiques,
High Street, Much Hadham.
Tel: (027 984) 2007

Country Life Antiques,
33a High Street, Bushey.
Tel: 01.950 8575

Frenches Farm Antiques,
Tower Hill, Chipperfield,
Kings Langley.
Tel: (092 77) 65843

Graham Porter,
31 Whitehorse Street, Baldock.
Tel: (0462) 895351

Langley Antiques,
15 High Street, Kings Langley.
Tel: (092 77) 64417

Romic,
4 Evron Place, Hertford.
Tel: (0992) 552880

Royston Antiques,
29 Kneesworth Street, Royston.
Tel: (0763) 43876

Stevens Antiques,
41 London Road, St. Albans.
Tel: (0727) 57266

Sweeney-in-London,
10 Southfield, Welwyn Garden City.
Tel: (07073) 32074

The Aspidistra,
29 Sun Street, Hitchin.
Tel: (0462) 53817

Tim Wharton Antiques,
24 High Street, Redbourn.
Tel: (058 285) 4371

Humberside

Bell Antiques,
68 Harold Street, Grimsby.
Tel: (0472) 695110

Keith Miles Marketing Ltd.,
Milbourne Sandhome Landing,
Newport, Brough.
Tel: (0430) 40210

Paul Wilson,
Perth St. West, Hull.
Tel: (0482) 447923

Kent

Chris De La Warre,
Crit Hall Farm, Benenden.
Tel: (0580) 240450

Clive D. Cowell,
Green Lane Farm, Bethersden.
Tel: (023 382) 382

Garry Blanch, Mounts Farm,
Benenden.
Tel: (0580) 240622

Scallywag, 22 High Street,
Beckenham.
Tel: 01.658 6633

Lancs.

Cardwell & Sheriff,
Moss Hey Garages, Chapel Road,
Morton Moss, Blackpool.
Tel: (0253) 696324

Didsbury Pine Centre,
King's Lynn Close, Didsbury,
Manchester.
Tel: (061 445) 4747

Enloc Antiques,
Old Corporation Yard,
Knotts Lane, Colne.
Tel: (0282) 861417

Gerry Haddock's Handmade
Furniture, The Covered Yard,
King Street, Lancaster.
Tel: (0524) 63404

Utopia Pine,
Holme Mills, Carnforth.
Tel: (0524) 781739

Leics.

Abbey Antiques,
Abbey Street, Market Harborough.
Tel: (0858) 62282

All Our Yesterdays,
19 London Road, Oadby.
Tel: (0533) 719049

Antique Emporium,
232 Narborough Road, Leicester.
Tel: (0533) 824942

Birches Antique Shop,
15 Francis Street, Stoneygate.
Tel: (0533) 703235

Carillon Antiques,
64 Leicester Road, Loughborough.
Tel: (0509) 37169

Christopher Roper's Pine Shop,
312 Welford Road, Leicester.
Tel: (0533) 704553

Country Antiques,
Main Street, Market Bosworth.
Tel: (0455) 291303

Curio Corner,
Market Street,
Ashby De La Zouch.
Tel: (0530) 413715

Interdecor,
10 High Street,
Market Harborough.
Tel: (0858) 66950

Kegworth Antiques,
Market Place, Kegworth.
Tel: (050 97) 2852

Kibworth Antique Centre,
Kibworth.
Tel: (053 753) 2761

Loughborough Antique Centre,
50 Market Street, Loughborough.
Tel: (0509) 39931

Lowe of Loughborough,
37-40 Church Gate, Loughborough.
Tel: (0509) 217876

Mawby's International,
Main Street, Churchover.
Tel: (0788) 832600

Nirvana Pine,
93 King Richards Road, Leicester.
Tel: (0533) 29304

Pine Supplies,
57 Hinckley Road, Leicester.
Tel: (0533) 541775

Quorn Pine,
12 High Street, Quorn.
Tel: (0509) 416031

Lincs.

Allens Antiques,
Moor Farm, Stapleford.
Tel: (052 285) 392

Antiques,
2 North Street, Gainsborough.
Tel: (0427) 4882

Dickenson & Thomas,
The Old Granary, 10 North Street,
Stamford.
Tel: (0780) 62236

Geoff Parker Antiques Ltd.,
The Chestnuts, Haltoft End,
Freiston, Nr. Boston.
Tel: (0205) 760444

Harwood Tate,
The Maltings, Serpentine Street,
Market Rasen.
Tel: (0673) 843579

Jim Baxter's Victorian Bazaar,
33 Wharf Road, Grantham.
Tel: (0476) 3977

Lawrence Shaw Antiques,
Spilsby Road, Horncastle.
Tel: (065 82) 7638

Mary King,
Victoria House, 2 Wargate Way,
Gosberton.
Tel: (0775) 840317

Michael Day Antiques,
North Street, Stamford.
Tel: (0733) 241842

P.D.R. Pine,
Oaklands, Ingoldsby.
Tel: (047 685) 400

Rudkin Antiques,
The Old School,
Station Road, Grantham.
Tel: (0476) 61477

Stowaway (U.K.) Ltd.,
2 Langton Hill, Horncastle.
Tel: (065 82) 7445

Tealby Pine,
Goltho Hall, Goltho,
Wragby, Nr. Lincoln.
Tel: (0673) 858789

Trevor Howsam Ltd.,
High Street, Kirton,
Nr. Boston.
Tel: (0205) 722595

Merseyside

Delta Antiques,
175-177 Smithdown Road,
Liverpool.
Tel: (051 734) 4277

Norfolk

Abbotts House Antiques,
25 White Hart Street, Aylsham.
Tel: (026 373) 4182

John Derham,
Earsham Hall, Earsham,
Nr. Bungay.
Tel: (0986) 3423

Northants

Acorn Antiques,
The Old Mill, Moat Lane,
Towcester.
Tel: (0327) 52788

Bits & Pieces,
34 High Street,
Higham Ferrers, Nr. Rushden.
Tel: (0933) 680430

Finedon Antique Centre,
3 Church Street, Finedon.
Tel: (0933) 680316

N. Long,
47 Bath Road, Kettering.
Tel: (0536) 521824

Richard Kimbell Antiques,
Harborough Road, Desborough.
Tel: (0536) 762041

Sheaf Street Antiques,
12a Sheaf Street, Daventry.
Tel: (032 72) 78126

The Antique Shop,
46 Bridge Street, Northampton.
Tel: (0604) 21983

The Old Buccluch,
46 The High Street,
Broughton, Nr. Desborough.
Tel: (0536) 790009

Village Antique Market,
62 High Street, Weedon.
Tel: (0327) 40766

Notts.

Alistair Fraser Antiques,
2a Rushworth Avenue,
West Bridgford.
Tel: (0602) 812782

Castle Antiques,
Bairds Malt, Northgate, Newark.
Tel: (0636) 704290

Corner House Antiques,
Farrar Close, Brunel Drive,
Northern Road Industrial Estate,
Newark.
Tel: (0636) 79014

Fine Pine,
69-73 Derby Road, Nottingham.
Tel: (0602) 413757

Jack Spratt Antiques,
5 Victoria Street, Newark.
Tel: (0636) 707714

Millbridge Pine,
60 Millgate, Newark.
Tel: (0636) 79637

R. A. Berry Antiques,
Manor Farm, Newark Road, Cotham,
Newark.
Tel: (0636) 71728

Top Hat,
Derby Road, Nottingham.
Tel: (0602) 49143

Vintage Pine,
113 Ilkeston Road, Nottingham.
Tel: (0602) 702571

Yesterday's Pine,
The Mill, Beehive Street, Retford.
Tel: (0777) 706256

Oxon.

Long Hanborough Antiques,
Long Hanborough.
Tel: (0993) 991484

Market Place Antiques,
35 Market Place,
Henley-on-Thames.
Tel: (049 12) 2387

Old Noah Antiques,
Chapel Square, Deddington.
Tel: (0869) 38259

Pine & Country Antiques,
28 Church Street,
Shipston-on-Stour.
Tel: (0608) 62168

Pine & Country Furniture,
4 West Street, Chipping Norton.
Tel: (0451) 31183

The Farmhouse, The Fourth Avenue,
Covered Market, Oxford.
Tel: (0865) 247084

Shropshire

Stripped Pine,
14 High Street, Ellesmere.
Tel: (069 171) 2717

Somerset

Domus,
Woodcock Street,
Castle Cary.
Tel: (0963) 50912

David & Penny Newlove Antiques,
28 High Street, Wincanton.
Tel: (0963) 32672

Genges Farm Antiques,
Limington, Nr. Yeovil.
Tel: (0935) 840464

Grange Court Antiques,
Corfe, Taunton.
Tel: (082 342) 498

Herald House, Antiques,
North Street, Langport.
Tel: (0458) 250587

Ilchester Antiques,
Church Street, Ilchester.
Tel: (0935) 841212

Milverton Antiques,
Fore Street, Milverton, Taunton.
Tel: (0823) 400597

Pennard House,
East Pennard, Shepton Mallet.
Tel: (074 986) 266

Steve Hales,
c/o Genges Farm, Limington,
Nr. Yeovil.
Tel: (0935) 840464

Staffs.

Anvil Antiques,
Old Step Row & The Old School,
Alsop Street, Leek.
Tel: (0538) 371657

Aspleys Antiques,
Compton Mill, Compton, Leek.
Tel: (0538) 373396

Stone-Wares,
The Stripped Pine Shop,
24 Radford Street, Stone.
Tel: (0785) 815000

Suffolk

Michael Moore Antiques,
The Old Court,
Nethergate Street, Clare.
Tel: (0787) 277510

Pine & Country Furniture,
Hacheston, Nr. Wickham Market.
Tel: (0728) 746485

Surrey

Knightsbridge Antiques,
43c Chipstead Valley Road,
Coulsdon.
Tel: 01.668 0148

Village Pine,
32 West Street, Farnham.
Tel: (0252) 726660

Wych House Antiques,
Wych Hill, Woking.
Tel: (048 62) 64636

Sussex

Hillside Antiques,
Balcombe Road, Pound Hill,
Crawley.
Tel: (0293) 883379/884018

Graham Price Antiques,
A27 Antiques Warehouse,
Dittons Road Industrial Estate,
Polegate.
Tel: (03212) 7167/7166

Pine & Country Antiques,
Sandhill Barn,
Washington.
Tel: (0903) 892888

Pine & Design,
Balcombe.
Tel: (044 483) 700

Rope Walk Antiques,
Rope Walk, Rye.
Tel: (0797) 223486

Victorian Pine Interiors,
12 Boundary Road, Hove.
Tel: (0273) 423384

Warwicks

Abode, The Shrieve House,
40 Sheep Street, Stratford.
Tel: (0789) 68755

Acorn Antiques,
17 Port Street, Evesham.
Tel: (0386) 49288

Antique Centre,
Railway Terrace, Rugby.
Tel: (0788) 62837

Ashworth's Country Workshop,
Snitterfield, Stratford-upon-Avon.
Tel: (0789) 731703/842071

J. Kilom Antiques,
16 Daventry Road, Dunchurch.
Tel: (0788) 817147

Stratford Antique Centre,
60 Ely Street, Stratford.
Tel: (0789) 204180

The Old Pine Seller,
17 Smith Street, Warwick.
Tel: (0926) 492151

The Old Rectory Country Furniture,
The Old Rectory, Loxley,
Nr. Stratford-upon-Avon.
Tel: (0789) 840254

West Midlands

Etcetra,
2 Poplar Road, Dorridge.
Tel: (056 45) 2192

Genesis,
222 Alcester Road,
Moseley, Birmingham.
Tel: (021 449) 8820

Pine Craft,
Unit 4, Station Road,
Rowley Regis, Birmingham.
Tel: (021 561) 3514

Ingrestre Antiques,
60 Belwell Lane, Four Ooaks,
Sutton Coldfield.
Tel: (021 308) 5453

Martin Quick Ltd.,
323 Tettenhall Road,
Wolverhampton.
Tel: (0902) 754703

Sylvia Ann Antiques,
Gazette Buildings,
164 Corporation Street, Birmingham.
Tel: (021 236) 2479

Victoriana,
101 North Road, Harborne.
Tel: (021 454) 1247

Wilts.

Jose Hornsey Antiques,
3 Silver Street,
Bradford-on-Avon.
Tel: (022 16) 4333

North Wilts Exporters,
Farm House, Brinkworth.
Tel: (066 641) 423

Ray Coggins Antiques,
The Old Brewery, Newtown,
Bradford-on-Avon.
Tel: (022 16) 3431

N. Yorks

Antique Pine,
Yorkshire Stripping Service,
Mill Farm, Kirk Hammerton, York.
Tel: (0901) 30451

Daleside Antiques,
4 St. Peter Square,
Cold Bath Road, Harrogate.
Tel: (0423) 60286

Old Rectory Antiques,
The Old Rectory,
West Heslerton, Malton.
Tel: (094 45) 364

Pine Finds,
The Old Cornmill,
Bishop Monkton, Harrogate.
Tel: (0765) 87159

Pond Cottage Antiques,
Brandsby Road, Stillington.
Tel: (0347) 810796

Swiftstrip/Studio Antiques,
Gallowfields Trading Estate,
Richmond.
Tel: (0833) 40809/(0748) 3556

S. Yorks

Mark Pidd Antiques,
190b Rockingham Street, Sheffield.
Tel: (0742) 383064

Peter James Antiques,
168 & 170 Devonshire Street,
Sheffield.
Tel: (0742) 700273

W. Yorks

Aberford Antiques,
Hicklam House, Aberford,
Nr. Leeds.
Tel: (0532) 813209

Antique Pine,
The Rookery, Salter Hebble, Halifax.
Tel: (0422) 45445

Hebble Furniture Limited,
Phoebe Lane Mills,
Phoebe Lane, Halifax.
Tel: (0422) 45445

J.V.T. Antiques,
80a Old Main Street, Bingley.
Tel: (0274) 566188

Manor Barn Pine,
Burnside Mill, Main Street,
Addingham, Ilkley.
Tel: (0943) 830176

Scar Top Antiques,
Far Scar Top,
Stanbury, Nr. Keighley.
Tel: (0535) 42585

Ireland

Alain Chawner,
The Square, Collom, Co. Louth.
Tel: (010 353) 4126270

Kilronan Antiques,
Kilronan, Cloghran, Co. Dublin.
Tel: (0001) 403499

Shamrock Antiques Ltd.,
Killaney, Ballina, Co. Mayo.
Tel: (010 353) 96-36275

Wales

Country Antiques,
The Bridge & Old Castle Mill,
Kidwelly, Dyfed.
Tel: (0554) 890534

Gladstone House Antiques,
Manod Old School,
Blaenau Ffestiniog, Gwynedd.
Tel: (0286) 2609

James & Pat Ash,
The Warehouse,
5 Station Road, Llandeilo, Dyfed.
Tel: (0558) 823726

14

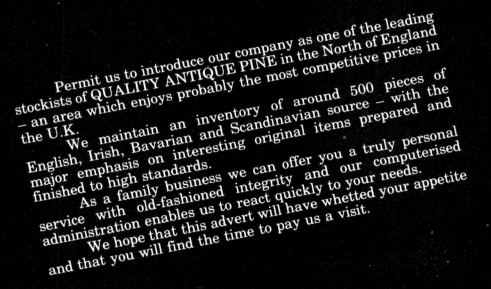

Pine & Country Furnit

The combined stock of the 6 dealers on this page represents one of the most interesting selections of English, Irish, Welsh and European pine & country furniture. Also French Provincial, original painted furniture, decorative items, metalwork and treen. All finished sympathetically to a very high standard. Deliveries can be arranged anywhere in the British Isles. Also container and packing service can be arranged locally.

e in Dorset & Somerset

● BATH

1
● MILVERTON

● TAUNTON

3 & 4
● ILCHESTER

2 ● CORFE

5 ● SHERBORNE

●
EXETER

● BEAMINSTER
6

1 MILVERTON ANTIQUES
Fore St, Milverton, Taunton, Somerset. Tel. 0823-400597.
Finely finished pine, period country furniture, unusual items including long case clocks.

2 GRANGE COURT ANTIQUES (Mr. & Mrs. Hawker)
Corfe, Taunton, Somerset. Tel. 0823-42-498
Good selection of English country pine, specialising in Welsh & West Country furniture & treen. Large showrooms.

3 GENGES FARM ANTIQUES (Roy & Pam Gilbert)
Showroom – Church St, Ilchester, Somerset. Tel. 0935-841212.
Home & Workshop – Genges Farm, Limington, Nr Ilchester, Somerset. Tel. 0935-840464
Good selection of 18th & 19th century English, Irish, Welsh and Continental pine & country furniture. Also original painted and French Provincial furniture and decorative items.

4 ILCHESTER ANTIQUES (Ron Oram)
Church St, Ilchester, Somerset. Tel. 0935-841212
Country pine furniture, metalwork, farm implements and tools and decorative items.

5 COUNTRY PINE & ANTIQUES (Simon & Tracey Dodge)
3 The Green, Sherborne, Dorset. Tel. 0935-815216
Good quality English, Irish & Continental pine furniture.

6 DANIELS HOUSE ANTIQUES (Carl & Gloria Hennessy)
Daniels House, Hogshill St, Beaminster, Dorset. Tel. 0308-862635.
Good selection of 18th & 19th century English, Irish, Welsh & Continental pine & country furniture. Also original painted, French Provincial & decorative items.

21

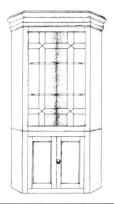

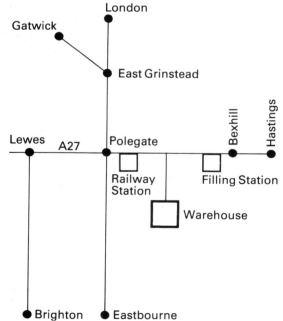

WOOD LOVES

BRIWAX

...naturally

The blend of natural waxes in BRIWAX put goodness and lasting protection into both old and new wood.

Ideal for Pine or Oak, the natural beeswax content will bring a natural shine and enhance any piece of furniture, whilst the carnuaba wax provides a hard surface. Just two reasons why it is the natural choice of professional craftsmen all over the world.

By appointment to H M Queen Elizabeth II
Manufacturers of polishes and lacquers

Available in clear or six wood shades. Packed into 450ml standard tins and 3.55 or 5 litre trade packs.

HENRY FLACK (1860) LTD
PO BOX 78 · BECKENHAM · KENT
Telephone: 01 658 2299 Telex: 946804 Facsimile: 01 658 8672

25

Restored Pine
AT
SCAR TOP ANTIQUES

Tim & Sandie Johnston

18th – 19th – 20th Century Pine restored by our own craftsmen with the emphasis on quality & originality.

Situated on the borders of Yorkshire and Lancashire we have a source of pine – infinite in variety and renowned for quality.

From the surrounding mills we stock weavers tables – leather workers donkeys – hide buckets – crackets – baskets – desks – etc.

Irish Pine – Extensive Range – dressers – food cupboards – tables – washstands – mirror backs – etc.

Continental Pine – Always readily available – plus our own reproduction lines – trestle tables, racks, etc.

Stripping plant – *stripping service provided*
Ebor Mill Ebor Lane
Haworth 44195

Warehouse & Container Bay
Moor Lodge
Stanbury

Showrooms & Workshops
Far Scar Top
Stanbury Keighley W. Yorks

Open: Weekdays 9am – 5pm   Weekends 1pm – 5pm or by appointment
Haworth 42585

27

Introduction

When we published our first *Pine Furniture Buyer's Price Guide* three years ago, we said then that pine furniture was coming into its own. It was no longer to be regarded as something good enough only as a carcase for a finer piece, as a mere copying wood to be disguised as something grander, or – in its raw state – fit only for playrooms and the like.

We said too that although some dealers dismissed its popularity then as a mere passing fad, we felt pine furniture was here to stay as something to be sought after – and that prices would continue to rise at the same rate as other antiques.

And we've been proved right. In fact, in the three years since then, shops dealing solely in pine have sprung up all over the country, the export trade is booming, and a whole new batch of associated interior decorating industries associated with pine have grown up. There are now shops that provide a design service for your home working with predominantly old pine, and there are places selling whole associated ranges of fabrics and objects designed or specially chosen to go with the pine look.

No longer the poor relation to other woods traditionally held in high esteem, pine is being restored, reproduced – even faked. The older and very attractive pieces can command very high prices, but it's worth remembering that there are still bargains to be had which will almost inevitably benefit your pocket in the long run if you look around for them.

What's the reason for this mini boom? First of all, collecting antiques of any sort of a reasonable quality is worthwhile. Not only is it fun, it can cost no more than buying new and, what's more, you're getting a 'one off'.

Besides that, antiques do represent an investment. And although for the average buyer, hoping to make immediate profits is out of the question and best left to the expert dealer, if you buy antiques wisely you will probably see your money returned after a few years – and you might even make a bit more on top. (The reason for the time gap, is because a dealer sells to you with his mark-up added on, so unless you were lucky or shrewd enough to spot an absolute bargain,

it will take a while for the piece to have appreciated sufficiently to cover that mark-up.) New goods, of course, don't rise in price – they drop to second hand value.

Why do antiques usually appreciate? First, because of their scarcity value. There aren't enough pieces around to meet demand, and the number of antiques from any period can only decline. Then the quality of materials and the workmanship tends to be better in old pieces than it does in today's mass produced goods. Superb quality stuff is still made today, of course, but because of the high cost of materials and skilled labour, it tends to be horribly expensive – and out of the reach of most pockets.

If you follow our advice and guidance, you'll be buying fairly

safely and in a recognised market – nevertheless, a safe rule to avoid disappointment is to buy only what you like. It's you who will have to see it every day, and a piece that irritates you fairly soon after you've got it home rarely grows on you. That's why it's important to look around carefully and familiarise yourself with antiques before you start shelling out on them.

As with planning any interior design scheme, and buying furniture to go with it, you must decide what you really like before going after it. It's all too easy to choose one style, have a change of mind, pick another – then wonder just why your house looks like a scene setting for *Steptoe and Son*. Few people can get the eclectic look right unless they're gifted with an exceptionally good eye. Not that that means you can't mix periods successfully, or that you can't put old with new to good effect.

Which brings us to another reason why pine is so popular these days. The beauty of any solid wood has its own timeless, classless, universal appeal, and stripped pine in particular is an attractive timber. It's also very easy to work with when it comes to decor. It has a warm golden glow that doesn't overpower and dominate a room as many of the darker woods do – rather it blends in and enhances the colours in a scheme.

And because much of what's available is nineteenth century, with some eighteenth and twentieth as well, it's an ideal choice where you're designing a house to take it back as closely as possible to its original period style.

Nevertheless, because most of the designs were never intended to be fashionable, but rather were workmanlike, usable pieces, around for years, they're not stuck rigidly in one period: they're versatile, looking as good in a predominantly modern period (think Habitat and Designers Guild) as in a genuinely old fashioned one.

It's this functionalism too that makes it so versatile – and pine furniture can live as happily in the kitchen or bathroom as the sitting room or bedroom. Thus you can achieve a continuity of decor in the house, build up a very personalised look – and never have to be afraid that the line will be discontinued.

But then, of course, where stripped pine furniture really comes into its own is where you want a country-cottage-even-in-town look. Many of the pieces were built for country houses – and their rustic simplicity and beauty is very seductive these days now the appeal of formica, melamine, chrome and plastics is waning. Then again, and perhaps even more interesting to those who like to keep up to the very latest developments in design, pine lends itself beautifully to being painted, using special antique techniques such as dragging, sponging, stippling and the like, or to being hand stencilled or painted with scenes.

Many of the early nineteenth century pieces of pine were painted – usually with pale green or blue milk paints (ie the pigments mixed with a base of skimmed milk or buttermilk), and often enriched with floral scenes and gilt. Or it might have been painted to simulate other woods: bambooing was popular, for instance. Or perhaps interest was added by lining drawer fronts, panels, legs with freehand stripes drawn around and down them.

If you pick up a piece bearing any of this work, it's usually worth keeping, because it's highly collectable. It might even be worth restoring. Wash the piece down with a mild soap solution – don't let it get too wet – then give it a coat of wax to see how the colours come up.

If it does need some restoration work, your local dealer might be able to recommend you to an artist who tackles this sort of thing. Or you could write to Rosie Fisher of Dragons of Walton St. Ltd, 23 Walton St., London SW3. (Tel: 01-589 3795/0548). She runs an interior design service which originally grew from selling painted antique furniture, and now has a team of highly skilled artists working for her who will undertake to paint items and interiors to special order.

Of course, you might feel brave enough to have a stab at doing the piece yourself – might, indeed, fancy creating something brand new, from scratch. Rosie Fisher's book *Rooms to Grow Up In* (Oct 84, Ebury Press, £7.95) explains the mysteries of specialist paint techniques, and shows how to do hand-painted designs. While *Paint Magic* by Jocasta Innes, has long been a bible for explaining old and new paint techniques. Try some of them out, you might be surprised at just how easy they are and how good they look.

What is pine?

Wood is normally divided into hardwood and softwood for the purposes of classification. The former usually comes from broad-leafed trees that shed their foliage in winter. Softwood comes from coniferous trees which don't shed their leaves.

These have traditionally been the least expensive timber for household joinery and included in this category are spruce, Douglas fir, eastern redwood and eastern and western pine. All softwoods are popularly and loosely called pine. Deal, by the way, is pine.

They're fine textured, close grained woods. The pine we normally see is pale gold, maturing to warm honey brown. Knots are dotted through the wood and the grain swirls around these. The wood is given a striped appearance by the annual growth rings: dark, hard stripes represent winter growth; light soft stripes represent summer growth. Therefore the most durable pine is that which grows in the harshest conditions, with a short summer to limit the growth of soft wood and increase the proportion of hard. This makes it more resistant to scratching and denting. And yet, it's because its fairly soft and easy to work with that carpenters have often been inspired to treat it to the sort of carving not often found in hardwood: many old pieces of pine are ornamented with beautiful carving, fretwork or turning.

These days, with the growing acceptance of pine as a valid wood even by the most diehard of conservative experts, the best pieces can be classed as 'fine' – though perhaps they can never be fine in the same way as classic mahogany or walnut. But then, it was never meant to be, and to try to see it as such is perhaps to miss its point – and to miss its charm.

Broadly speaking there are three types of British pine furniture: country pieces made by local craftsmen, such as cupboards, tables, chairs, chests and coffers. These would most characteristically have been left in their natural state and would be cared for by scrubbing or waxing. Then there was late Victorian mass-produced furniture, made to meet the requirements of a new and wealthy middle class who wanted furniture for the kitchen, the maid's bedroom and the nursery. So chests of drawers, sideboards, wardrobes, dressing tables and washstands, dressers, cupboards and chiffoniers were all turned out, often to be painted, stained or veneered. Pine was frequently used as a copying wood. And finally, there were architectural fittings for fairly grand houses: bookcases and shelves, barrel backed corner cupboards, fine fire surrounds and the like. Often they were designed especially to fit with the style of the rooms they were intended for, and would be painted to match the decor. Unfortunately,

A complete continental apothecary's shop interior, decorated with painted pine including 35 ft of shelving and counter. MPA

much of this last category has been broken up or burned when these houses were converted and modernised. But it's still possible to find pretty pine fireplaces, if you're determined.

Furniture from all three categories is likely to be found in almost any condition – from the pitifully dilapidated, through the cunningly concealed and camouflaged, to the carefully preserved or restored and beautifully kept. Remember too that the original quality of pine furniture does vary a good deal – some was hastily nailed together, some truly skilfully built. And because a good deal of it was meant to be painted, sometimes construction details were treated less carefully – and dowels or pegs might appear at every joint when the piece is stripped, or filler might cover nailheads. Still, these things are thought to add to its rustic, authentic charm.

How are you likely to find your pine furniture? Unless it has already been stripped, or indeed, has always been in its natural state, you're likely to find your potential piece of beautiful, natural pine, hidden beneath paint, black fake ebony varnish, or a dull and dirty brown varnish. Or all or some of these of course.

The important thing is to find out what the bottom layer is. Do this by scratching and flaking off a bit in a part that's hidden with a key or a coin. If the wood shows clear – fine. But if a red stain is visible, then beware. It's likely to be the penetrating pigment of an old brown stain or paint. And it's difficult to remove. It could always be given a new paint job, or the stain itself *can* be minimised (see below). The effort might be worth it if you particularly want the piece for its shape, rather than what you visualised as a warm blond natural wood finish. It does probably mean though, you'll be able to get the piece cheaper.

How do you date pine?

Dating pine is difficult, because it was used so much in functional furniture whose styles changed little over the years. Added to this, the usual dating guides will often have been replaced. Thus original wooden or porcelain handles may have been replaced by modern brass – or even modern porcelain! – handles. And original bun feet might have been replaced by bracket feet or a brass or wooden plinth.

Look in drawer fronts and cupboard doors – if there are holes, then the handles have probably been changed. In the middle of the nineteenth century nails, screws and dovetail joints were usually machine made – so if nails and screws are rough and wavy, and dovetail joints are irregular, then chances are the piece was made before mid-nineteenth century. The wood will look hand planed too. You'll have to look for these details: by their very nature, they'll be hidden.

It's worth carrying out a few checks before parting with your cash. Stripping pine in a caustic solution can loosen joints, so check that arms, legs and splats are all stable. Because pine is soft, feet and cornices have often been lost over the years, so check the new additions are satisfactory: the colour must match, the workmanship should be good – the joints should not be just nailed or screwed together. Bureaux are often composed of old chests of drawers: a telltale sign is that when you look at the bureau lid and desk interior, the wood will feel different and the interior will be too new. The cost of a made up bureau is lower than an original. With a chest of drawers, you need to know that the drawers run smoothly, the drawer back stops are in place so drawers don't disappear to the back, and that the handles are of good quality.

None of this matters that much, of course, if you're buying cheaply and you know what you're getting. But if you're spending quite a lot of money, then you want the best value. It helps to know what you're looking at in an auction or in a country market. But if you're buying from a reputable dealer, then he or she should be able to guide you on price and condition.

Buying

Like any other retailer, an antique dealer is in business to make a profit. And, despite widely held notions about the vast amounts of money they're supposed to make, many of them have had a struggle to keep in business during the recession. And, while the pound has held strong, many foreign buyers haven't been coming over as much as they used to. A dealer can only sell his stock for what the market will pay. And competition from other dealers and the fact that *anyone* can bid at an auction (often against dealers) keeps prices down. Still, when times aren't so hot for dealers, it's a good time for the private buyer to invest.

The best dealers are experts with a fund of knowledge and at the highest level, they advise salerooms and museums. In the middle range, they will still be knowledgeable and are usually happy to talk to you about their stock: everyone likes to cultivate potential customers who will keep coming. At the lower level – say with country markets and the like – you'll often find people who are doing it as a hobby or just starting off in the antique world who might only know as much – less even – than the average buyer. Though that's not to say there aren't plenty of people who know what they're talking about with a market stall.

There's no one price for any antique. That's why prices fluctuate – even in the same shop. If he can't sell an item, a dealer will often lower the price. Discounts are normally given to the trade. That's why many shops don't have price tags showing, but rather a code which is usually in two parts: a target price for a fellow dealer and a target price for a private buyer.

VAT quite often isn't included in the quoted price – so ask what the total would be.

People are often daunted at the thought of going into an antique shop – particularly fairly upmarket ones. Don't be. All you have to do is to use your common sense and follow a few sensible rules. Even those shops marked 'trade only' would welcome plausible customers if they were approached in the right way.

I used to work in an antique shop, so I know a few of the things that set a dealer's teeth on edge. Don't go in with a brood of children who will undoubtedly run round, knock things over and pick things up. Don't treat a shop as a museum, asking questions about everything with no intention of buying – particularly if the dealer is busy with some for-real customers. Don't use it simply as a handy place to shelter from the rain. Don't keep asking the price of things, then say you've got one just like that at home. If the dealer is involved with some heavy bargaining from a foreign exporter, don't keep interrupting.

Above: A private pine collector's room tastefully furnished. By courtesy of Jose Hornsey.

Right Centre: A charming room setting enhanced by pictures and personal belongings. By courtesy of Pine & Design.

What you can do though is ask sensible questions about the sort of things you are buying. If you can't see what you want, ask. A piece of pine might be being stripped next door, or the dealer could be expecting a new delivery of stock which might furnish what you want. If you develop a good relationship and he or she comes to know your taste, they might even ring you to tell you something of interest has come in. You can always ask if a price is the best that can be done, but it's insulting to keep bargaining – no-one sells for less than they think is justified. (Though in a market, it's the bargaining that often makes for the fun.) It's probably best to deal in cash because large cheques have to be cleared. And have transport ready to take your purchase away. Always ask for a receipt with the price paid written on it and the dealer's description of what you've bought.

Buying at Auction

Buying from a dealer is perhaps the easiest way of acquiring your pieces, but as you become more knowledgeable, salerooms and auctions represent an alternative source – and a lot of fun they are too. Buying at auction is exciting – and a taste you can get hooked on.

Don't be put off by the idea there's some mystery about it. You won't be lumbered with some esoteric and wildly expensive item you've never set eyes on just because you blew your nose or coughed in the middle of the proceedings.

There are four big London salerooms: Christie's, Sotheby's, Phillips, and Bonhams. Write to them or ring for details about their forthcoming sales of pine furniture (addresses below). And there are plenty of country salerooms that usually advertise in the local paper

VAT and any buyer's commission. You'll probably find here too a disclaimer saying the auctioneer isn't responsible in any way for the authenticity and quality of the piece. So you must examine those items you're interested in during viewing hours, they're usually the morning of the sale or the day before. If you still have doubts, then ask the advice of the auctioneer.

Get to the sale in good time. Then, when you want to bid, make a clear sign – raise your catalogue decisively, for instance. After that, don't fidget and keep the signs clear, because once he's aware you're in the running, the auctioneer will be looking to you to make a bid. Don't be tempted to go over your personal limit in the heat of the moment – you should have written it beside the lot number to help you stick with it. If you want to get out of the running, shake your hand firmly when the auctioneer next looks to you to make an offer.

If you do buy, you'll be expected to take your piece away quickly. If you can't do this yourself, you'll have to pay for transport and the auctioneer is entitled to charge you for storage.

Other good sources of bargain pine finds are local markets. Ask around for where and when they're held – for instance, there's a good one on Saturday morning in Brighton around the Gardener Street area, but you have to get there about 6.30 to beat the dealers. Then there are municipal dumps where literally anything can turn up; demolition sites and house conversions (ask the foreman if there's anything for sale); and the classified sales pages in local papers can sometimes be fruitful. And, of course, ask older relatives if they've got any old wooden junk they don't want and which might well be pine. They might not have seen it's potential when it's stripped – but you will.

Top Left: Fabric and wallpaper complete the picture in this lady's boudoir providing the grace and elegance of a bygone age. By courtesy of Pine & Design.

Left: The four-poster bed 1980-style – no longer the uncomfortable box of our Victorian forebears – with all-enclosing drapes. Here the golden pine wood is enhanced with delicate cotton fabric. By courtesy of Pine & Design.

Above: A pine sideboard – a most useful piece of furniture presented here with a fine carved mirror above, useful and beautiful it would surely look at home in the finest residence. By courtesy of Pine & Design.

– a sale of "Antique and Other Furniture and Effects" would probably be nicely junky, ripe for picking up bargains.

An auctioneer is an agent whose job it is to raise the highest price he can for the seller, then he takes his commission. Sometimes a buyer's commission is charged as well. Check the auction room's conditions of sale carefully – they'll be in the catalogue of each sale. And when doing your financial calculations, remember to include not only the hammer price, but also

Stripping Off

If you've got a piece of pine that needs stripping, you can either have it professionally treated, or do it yourself. A professional will dip it in a tank of chemical stripping solution, clean and dry it and do any necessary restoration work. Modern methods have much improved over recent years and the days of a piece coming apart in the tank is a thing of the past. And it's the care and expertise of commercial stripping firms that's responsible for the popularity of pine, and the wealth and variety of it that's around. Your local dealer might be able to recommend a good stripper, if not, look in the Yellow Pages under **Cabinet Makers** for people likely to tackle this kind of work.

On the other hand, you might enjoy the thought of stripping a piece yourself, or it might be too small – a box, say – that isn't worth sending off. Or, of course, you might be stripping door or window frames. Pat Cutforth's book: *Stripping Pine and Other Woods* is out in paperback, is published by John Murray, and costs £4.95. In it she gives the whole low down on stripping, treating and maintaining pine – and it's excellent stuff for if you really get hooked on the whole business.

Meanwhile, here's one standard method of stripping off old paint and varnish:

Before you start

1 Work in the open or a very well ventilated area – the fumes can overpower.
2 Protect everything – tough rubber gloves on your hands, a thick overall for clothes. Stripper burns so if you do come into contact, wash it off immediately.
3 Put thick layers of newspaper all around to guard against drips and splashes.
4 Remove metal fittings.
5 Go slowly, tackle one patch at a time and finish each properly

before going onto the next.
6 Do everything *with* the grain – the tool will sink in otherwise. This rule is broken though when tackling the grooves of a turned leg.
7 Test on an out of the way patch first.

Tools and materials

1 Stripper – read manufacturer's instructions to make sure you're buying enough. A jellied one will be easier to work with on verticals and one that can be removed with white spirit rather than water is a good choice, because water raises the grain.
2 Metal scraping knives.
3 Medium grade steel wool.
4 An old paint brush.
5 A metal container for scraping paint into.
6 White spirit.
7 Clean rags.
8 Clean water in case of accidents.
9 Toothbrush or manicurist's orange stick.

Method

Read instructions first to see if there are any variations or extras on this basic method. Wipe piece over with white spirit to remove any wax. Brush stripper on thickly and leave till paint bubbles. Push some paint aside with a scraper to see if the bare wood is visible. If it is, or if the stripper has stopped working anyway, carefully scrape off the gunge into the container. Re-apply stripper to stubborn areas of paint. Don't dig and scrape or you'll damage the timber. When the surface layers have gone, dip some of the wire wool in the stripper and rub down, discarding each piece in the container as it clogs. Treat mouldings, ruts and grooves with an orange stick or toothbrush so you don't damage.

When all your paint and varnish is removed, do a final clean: apply white spirit with wire wool, and then with a clean cloth, and keep going until all traces of stripper have gone.

Soak metal fittings – hinges and handles – in a jar of liquid stripper, and when the paint has dissolved, rinse and dry.

Below: A garden setting for lazy hazy summer days – is there no end to its uses. Once again the golden tones of pine blend perfectly on the patio or in the garden. By courtesy of Pine & Design.

Right: A range of craftsman's tools presents an attractive picture. By courtesy of Pine & Design.

Finishing

The best way of finishing pine is a controversial subject and in the end you'll have to rely on personal judgement and taste, though if you're really unsure, ask the advice of your local dealer.

First, assess the condition of your stripped piece. Scratches can be carefully sanded out, widening the surrounding area to blend in. Always sand in the direction of the grain. Dents can be smoothed by placing a damp cloth over them and warming with an iron. Burns can be sanded out and filled if necessary. You can fill with wax – dripped from a candle – or a proprietary stopper.

Next comes sanding which paradoxically both smooths down the surface and roughens it – keys it up to take a finish. Use a medium grade like F2 then move onto fine – grade 1 – to finish. When you're satisfied, dab a wet finger on the

Above: A kitchen furnished with pieces of antique pine, simple, practical and homely, a perfect setting for cotton fabrics. With today's modern culinary aids we have indeed the best of both worlds. By courtesy of Laura Ashley.

Right: The Welsh Dresser, the most popular item of all pine furniture. Conjuring up pictures of memories long ago – farmhouse holidays, country fare, plates and dishes, what better way to display your favourite china. By courtesy of Pine & Design.

wood – that's roughly how it will look when polished. If you like the colour, fine. If you don't, you can change it.

If you want to lighten it or minimise a red stain you can bleach your piece with ordinary household bleach applied with a sponge. Again work in a well ventilated area. A couple of applications should do the trick. If it doesn't try a proprietary two part bleach – Rustins do one – but the effect is fairly drastic so be warned. If you want to darken it, use a wood stain. These products are all available at hardware stores. As always test on hidden spot first.

Now you're ready for finishing and waxing. Many pine dealers apply wax straight onto the bare wood and of course, you can do the same. But this doesn't give resistance to stains, spills and heat, so furniture intended for practical use in a family home should perhaps be given a finish that gives some measure of protection before waxing.

Where you need something that's hard wearing, heat and moisture proof, a polyurethane sealer or a polyurethane varnish is a good solution. A sealer is absorbed into the wood, a varnish sits on top. For furniture a matt finish thinned 10% with white spirit is a good sealer. A good wax polish will mellow the appearance and give protection. If the surface is to take some *very* hard wear – kitchen work tops, for instance – a two part polyurethane varnish will give very effective protection. For something that's mostly decorative and won't receive much wear you can use the minimal seal of shellac – namely, French polish. This can be bought

from hardware stores. Follow manufacturer's instructions.

Whatever you've used, the final step is a good wax polish. You'll find anyway that once you've rubbed down the finish with finest gauge steel wool, you won't be able to tell one finish from another very easily – particularly after years of polishing. Apply polish sparingly, rubbing hard and working along the grain. To maintain, dust regularly and give another coat of polish occasionally.

N.B. – When carrying out any treatment, always read manufacturer's instructions if using a proprietary product. Always test first on an inconspicuous patch. Remember, that any treatments are carried out at your own risk.

Decorating with Pine

How do you use your pine furniture to best effect? It's not the individual pieces in a room that make up a look – it's more the way in which things are put together, the colours and the textures of the background, the different materials, and the accessories used to reinforce the style – the effect of the whole together is what counts.

Pine is a versatile wood whose pale gold tones complement many colour schemes. You don't have to be after a rustic feel to use it to good effect – after all, one chest does not a country cottage make. Use it in a bright and cheerful modern room teamed with primary colours, gingham curtains or fine blinds, white pottery and plenty of plants for an easy to live with look.

On the other hand, it's equally beautiful and gorgeously restful with pastel colours, fresh printed or plain glazed cottons, glass and porcelain displays and masses of flowers for a soothing, prettily feminine atmosphere.

But, if your aim is the country cottage feel, or you're after making an 18th or 19th century house look more as it used to be, then pine is an obvious choice. A rustic period feel is epitomised by a return to natural materials and textures and the use of simple and comfortable furniture.

So the natural tones of stripped pine or the gentle earthy tones of handpainted wood is mixed with natural flooring in stone, brick quarry tile, slate or stripped floorboards. Woodwork can be either painted a soft white or be stripped. Walls are brick, plaster, the palest creams or off-whites and sometimes ochre. Wallpaper can be used, usually in the bedroom, most often in small sprigged designs or prettily washed-out pastels. Windows are left bare or shuttered or hung with simple curtains, roller, Roman or festoon blinds – again in fresh florals, pale pastels or perhaps a natural calico. And old lace looks fabulous. Tables are good draped with a circle or two of fabric and arranged with a collection of porcelain, pictures or glass and bathed in a pool of soft light from a traditional table lamp. Rugs should be in natural earthy tones or warm pastels and they should pick up on the colours in the rest of the room. Period objects – pitchers and basins, pottery and porcelain, china plates and old prints for the walls, old books for shelves – all give the right feel. Scour your junk shops. Arrange plenty of cushions and pillows. Put out lots of vases of flowers. Bundle masses of dried flowers in baskets.

Bedrooms look authentic with four poster or brass beds, bathrooms are good with brass taps, natural sponges, old fashioned bottles of cologne and shaving accessories (Culpepper or Penhaligon bottles are pretty), and bowls of pot pourri. You can box in a bath or a sink with wood from an old wardrobe.

Modern kitchens are both workplaces and the hub of a home. When giving it a period feel, stick to the spirit rather than the letter. A natural stone or tile floor, a big kitchen table with simple chairs, benches or a pew, a dresser set with china are what's wanted. If you've got an Aga, so much the better. Keep solid cupboards below work surface level to hide clutter, put glazed cupboards or open shelves above to display pretty kitchen paraphernalia. You don't have to have a fitted kitchen: a mixture of furniture and some joinery works very well. Worktops should be made in pine or marble. Or you can have a kitchen custom built to your specifications by one of the new companies who work in old pine. Pine and Design (address below) is an interior design company who design and build kitchens, bedrooms and bathrooms in old pine and will undertake to do a complete back up service, supplying all the necessary accessories. And Antique Pine Partners design and build antique pine kitchens, bathrooms and bedroom and living areas. Their address is below. Finish off, of course, with assorted kitchenalia.

Christie's South Kensington Ltd.,
85 Old Brompton Road,
London SW7.
Tel: 01-581 2231.

Sotheby, Parke Bernet & Co.,
34 & 35 New Bond Street,
London W1.
Tel: 01-493 8080.

Phillips, Son & Neale,
Blenstock House,
7 Blenheim Street,
New Bond Street,
London W1.
Tel: 01-629 6602.

Bonhams,
Montpelier Galleries,
Montpelier Street,
Knightsbridge,
London SW7.
Tel: 01-584 9161.

Dressers

Pine dressers have seen a tremendous increase in value over the last five years. Good quality dressers of fine colour are very scarce and have seen a substantial price increase. Many of these dressers were destroyed in house renovations in the 50's and 60's and this scarcity, plus increased demand, has caused quite a few fakes to appear on the market.

The history of the dresser is indelibly linked to its utilitarian function. The earliest 'dresser' was a table set against a wall below shelves. This was the main area of food preparation. By the late seventeenth century the shelves and table had been combined, by the addition of a boarded back, into a single piece of furniture. They tended to be a particularly functional piece of furniture, which had little applied decoration. They often incorporated a potboard or cupboards below and the narrow shelves above were used for storage and/or display.

This display function led to the incorporation of many decorative embellishments. Early in the eighteenth century drawers were often added below the working surface and a simple cornice was the first of many decorative additions to adorn this very basic piece of furniture.

In the nineteenth century the dresser was an essential piece of furniture, either in the kitchen or in farmhouses and cottages as the perfect china cabinet and sideboard. This was the boom time for the dresser and the adage 'every home should have one' was certainly followed. Most of the dressers we find in antique shops today come from this period and the most desirable have applied mouldings and decorative turnings.

A Georgian pine Welsh 'dog kennel' dresser, 81in. high, 62in. wide. £500-600   Co

An English pine dresser, in original condition, 5ft. 6in. high, 6ft. 3in. wide, c.1740. £1,500-1,600   Jos

A late Georgian pine dresser, painted with deep coloured varnish. £1,800-2,000

A Georgian pine two-drawer dresser base, 70in. wide, 29in. deep, 29in. high. £250-275   PF

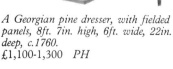

A Georgian pine dresser, with fielded panels, 8ft. 7in. high, 6ft. wide, 22in. deep, c.1760. £1,100-1,300   PH

A Georgian pine dresser, 6ft. 3in. high, 5ft. 2in. wide, 19in. deep, c.1730. £600-700   PH

A small dresser base, in pine and sycamore, 44in. wide, 31in. high, 22in. deep, c.1800. £300-350   PH

An English pine dresser base, with sycamore top, good moulding on drawers and doors, and excellent turnings for decoration, 7ft. wide, c.1810. £325-400   MB

A North Welsh pine dresser base, with a thick sycamore top, arched and moulded cupboard doors, 33in. high, 7ft. 6in. wide, 20in. deep, c.1800. £575-625   PH

There are features which give some clues as to the provenance of the dresser. When listing these it must be emphasised that styles were copied from one region to the next and these points are only indicators of the origin of the dresser.

WEST COUNTRY:

- glazed
- shelved cupboards above
- drawers and cupboards below
- usually quite decorative
- with bobbin and cotton-reel turned mouldings to sides, drawers and cornices

NORTH COUNTRY & MIDLANDS:

- often without rack shelves
- often with spice drawers at either end of a low backboard
- some larger examples have drawers in the base flanking a breakfront central cupboard
- many have side pillars in the base, decorated with applied split mouldings

SCOTTISH:

- mostly resemble chiffoniers
- have a row of spice drawers at the base of a low backboard
- often have cushion-moulded drawers above two or three cupboards
- stand on solid plinths or four turned feet

IRISH:

- close-boarded back to the rack shelves
- with shaped frieze to the cornice
- the base with three cupboards, or two cupboards flanking a fiddle front
- often crudely constructed
- with solid plinth or bracket feet

An original Welsh pine 'dog kennel' dresser, 7ft. high, 5ft. wide, c.1840. £550-650 RK

A Victorian pine dresser, in two pieces, with two drawers, two cupboards and boarded back, 79in. high, 47in. wide, 19in. deep. £350-400 AH

A pine dresser, 92in. high, 80in. wide, 17½in. deep, c.1840. £950-1,000 W

An 18th C. glazed pine dresser, with cupboards below, 74in. high, 41in. wide, 19in. deep. £230-300 GLF

A Lancashire pine dresser, with ogee bracket feet, 7ft. 5in. high, 5ft. 6in. wide c.1865. £750-800 HG

A pine dresser base, 3ft. high, 6ft. wide, 18in. deep. £140-200   DPN

An 18th C. pine dresser base, with replacement handles, 6ft. 6in. wide. £300-350   AL

A pine dresser base, 5ft. wide, c.1860. £185-250   UP

A 19th C. pine dresser, 76in. high, 47in. wide, 17in. deep. £230-275   GLF

An English pine dresser, 6ft. 10in. high, 4ft. 6in. wide. £400-450   GF

A West Country pine dresser of very small size, with dog tooth dentil cornice, 78½in. high, 52in. wide. £550-650   RC

A pine dresser, 73½in. high, 52in. wide, 18in. deep, c.1850. £330-400   WH

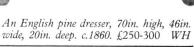

A long pine potboard dresser base, 37in. high, 11ft. 2in. wide, 22in. deep, c.1830. £625-675   PH

An English pine dresser, 70in. high, 46in. wide, 20in. deep. c.1860. £250-300   WH

An Irish pine dresser, 6ft. 6in. high by 4ft. 2in. wide, c. 1850. £385-400 UP

A Southern Irish pine dresser, converted to chicken coop, with plate rack above, 6ft. 6in. high, 4ft. wide, c.1850. £350-400 RK

An Irish pine cottage dresser, 48in. by 19in. by 71in., c.1850. £575-600 Bed

An Irish pine fiddle front dresser, 6ft. 6in. by 4ft., c. 1820. £385-400 UP

An Irish pine dresser, 6ft. 3in. by 4ft. 3in., c.1850. £275-325 RK

A Southern Irish pine dresser, 7ft. high, 5ft. wide, c.1840. £350-420 RK

A 19th C. Irish pine dresser, with two drawers, two doors and decorative cornice, 6ft. 2in. high, 4ft. wide. £440-475 DH

A 19th C. Irish pine dresser, with two drawers, two doors and decorative cornice, 7ft. high, 4ft. 4in. wide. £420-475 DH

An Irish decorated pine dresser, 6ft. 1in. high, 5ft. wide, c.1850. £500-600 HG

A late Victorian pine dresser, 83in. high, 53in. wide, 18in. deep. £725-775 W

An Irish pine dresser, in two sections, 80in. high, 48in. wide, c.1840. £420-460 AL

A pine chicken coop dresser, with original base, top replaced from old dresser, 6ft. 6in. high 4ft. 6in. wide, base, c. 1780. £400-450 HH

A primitive Southern Irish pine dresser, with heavy moulded decoration, 6ft. 6in. high by 4ft. 9in. wide, c.1860. £350-400 RK

A pine chicken coop dresser, with later top, 57in. wide, c. 1850. £1,500-1,800 Ad

*A Dublin pine dresser, 6ft. high by 3ft. 9 in. wide. £225-250 RK
Note that the top is original to the base.*

An early 19th C. Irish pine dresser, with breakfront cornice, in totally original condition, 7ft. 4in. high, 4ft. 10in. wide. £560-600 DH

An Irish pine dresser, with new handles, 4ft. wide, c.1840. £300-380 AL

An 18th C. Irish pine dresser, 77in. high, 48in. wide, 18in. deep. £320-375 GLF

An Irish pine dresser, 79in. high, 56in. wide, c.1780. £400-450 WH

A Southern Irish pine dresser, with unusual drawer arrangement, 7ft. high, 4ft. 9in. wide, c.1850. £330-360 RK

A Welsh pine dresser, with glazed top, 7ft. high, 6ft. wide, c. 1800. £750-795 MB

An East German pine dresser, the bottom is a cupboard which looks like a drawer base, 71in. high, 37in. wide, 20in. deep, c.1820. £275-325 WH

An East German pine glazed front china cabinet, 82in. high, 39in. wide, 19in. deep. £280-300 WH

A French pine panelled and glazed cupboard, 6ft. 3in. high, 3ft. 7in. wide, 21in. deep, c.1840. £250-300 PH

A Southern Irish pine dresser, converted to chicken coop, with plate rack above, the original dresser c.1840, 6ft. 6in. high, 4ft. wide. £300-400 RK

An Austrian pine glazed dresser, 80in. high, 43in. wide, 23in. deep, c.1875. £450-475 Bed

A late 19th C. pine glazed dresser/ bookcase, 6ft. 8in. high, 4ft. wide. £350-380 MV

An Austrian pine dresser, 78in. high, 43in. wide, 19in. deep. £475-500 Bed

A small pine dresser, 6ft. 4in. high, 3ft. 9in. wide, c.1800. £425-450 BEL

A German pine kitchen cabinet, with original ceramic spice drawers, 71in. high, c.1900. £250-350 WH

A 19th C. Cornish pine dresser, with split applied moulding, 79in. high, 54in. wide, 21in. deep. £300-325 PCo

A glazed top pine dresser, 82in. high, 54in. wide, 20in. deep. £300-325   DPN

A pine glazed dresser, recently painted, 6ft. 6in. high, 3ft. 7in. wide, c.1885. £300-325   BEL

A French pine glazed cupboard, 7ft. 2in. high, 3ft. 4in. wide, 17in. deep c.1870. £250-300   PH

An Edwardian pine glazed dresser, with three spice drawers, 44in. wide. £450-495   D

A 19th C. Irish pine dresser, with two drawers and two doors, with raised fielded panels, fretted cornice and removable plate bars, 6ft. 4in. high, 5ft. wide. £500-550   DH

A pine dresser, 6ft. high, 3ft. 10in. wide, £225-250   BEL

A pine dresser, with leaded glass, 68in. wide, c.1890. £275-350   W

A Cornish pine glazed dresser, 69in. high, 57in. wide, c.1865. £630-675 Bed

An Edwardian pine glazed dresser, 74in. high, 48in. wide, 20in. deep. £255-275   WH

47

A Victorian pine dresser, with original glass knobs, in very good order, 6ft. 8in. high, 5ft. wide, 18in. deep, c.1840. £500-650 SW

An Irish pine dresser, with reeded decoration, c.1820. £350-450 SAL

A Quicksey pine kitchen cabinet, complete with original fittings, glass storage jars and drawers, spice rack, flour bin and memoranda panels inside top doors, for shopping and useful household hints, enamel work top, 82in. high, 48in. wide, 22in. deep, early 1920's. £350-400 OC

An early 19th C. Irish pine dresser, with breakfront cornice and cotton-reel moulding to sides, 6ft. 3in. high, 4ft. 6in. wide. £500-550 PF

A small Victorian pine glazed dresser, with cupboards and drawers, in excellent condition, 6ft. 10in. high, 4ft. 6in. wide. £420-480 OPS

A 19th C. Scottish pine dresser, with applied bullseye moulding on the pediment and a bevelled mirror on the centre cupboard, 85in. high, 51in. wide, 20in. deep. £375-395

A 19th C. pine dresser, 85in. wide. £550-625 D

A Victorian glazed pine dresser, with arched glazed doors, shaped plinth, in excellent condition, 7ft. 2in. high, 7ft. wide, c.1850. £575-625 OPS

An early 20th C. English pine dresser, 77in. high, 54in. wide, 18in. deep. £375-400 Sca

A 19th C. pine dresser, 76in. high, 63in. wide. £450-475 Ad

A mid 19th C. pine dresser, 95in. high, 67in. wide. £550-595 Ad

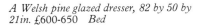

A Welsh pine glazed dresser, 82 by 50 by 21in. £600-650 Bed

A 19th C. pine dresser, 85in. high. £500-550 Ad

A Victorian pine dresser, with two drawers, moulded cupboard doors, 75in. high, 44in. wide, 24in. deep. £350-450 CRA

Sideboards and Chiffoniers

A natural progression from the dresser was the sideboard or chiffonier. This piece of pine furniture again started life as a functional copy of the much grander pieces made in oak and mahogany.

The sideboard was more suitable for use in the small cottages and farm-houses and housed most of the family's valuable possessions. As the nineteenth century progressed the plain style was superseded by a more elaborately decorated style. The sideboards also tended to be much larger to correspond with the general Victorian taste. The pine sideboard lost out in the battle against the mass-produced mahogany pieces but there are still large numbers available in both the polished and unstripped state. Do read our guide to stripping in the introduction before grabbing that tin of paint-stripper!

A Swedish pine sideboard, with mirror, 6ft. high, 4ft. 3in. wide. £400-450   BEL

A Victorian pine chiffonier, with carved back board and central mirror, standing on six turned feet, 68in. high, 60in. wide, 20in. deep. £400-450   *PJ*

An English pine sideboard, with mirror back, 65in. high, 61in. long, c.1910. £300-350   MB

An Edwardian pine credenza, with panelled cupboard doors and bun feet. £300-325   D

A 19th C. pine sideboard, with beaded and panelled doors and carved side pillars, 38in. high, 49in. wide, 20in. deep. £230-270

A small Scandinavian pine sideboard, with two drawers, 3ft. 1in. high, 4ft. 2in. wide, c.1875. £140-160   BEL

A pine buffet, 54in. high, 60in. wide, 22in. deep. £220-250   DPN

A Victorian pine sideboard, on six feet, with glass handles, 65in. £235-300

A Victorian pine sideboard, with seven drawers and centre cupboard, carved back, on bun feet, 43in. high, 61in. wide. £300-400   Ad

A late 19th c. pine chiffonier, (sideboard), with porcelain handles, 60in. high, 58in. wide. £290-325   *Ad*

A pine buffet, on bracket feet, 3ft. 3in. high, 5ft. 2in. wide, 20in. deep, c.1860. £300-400 HH

A Regency pine chiffonier, 3ft. 10in. wide, 2ft. deep, c.1820. £220-260 AL

A large Danish pine sideboard, with curved doors, 74in. wide, c.1890. £350-420 W

A Regency pine chiffonier, 47in. high, 36in. wide. £220-260 AL

A 19th C. pine chiffonier, 38in. high, 58in. wide. £200-250 Ad

A Lincolnshire carved pine chiffonier, 60in. wide. £300-340 D

A pine cupboard, with four doors, 35in. high, 72in. wide, 20in. deep. £150-200 DPN

A Lincolnshire pine chiffonier, 34½in. high, 59½in. wide, 22in. deep, c.1850. £385-400 Sca

A Welsh pine chiffonier, 66in. high, 58in. wide, 20½in. deep, c.1850. £450-500 Sca

A pine cupboard, with three drawers, 36in. high, 53in. wide. £180-200 DPN

A North Country pine chiffonier, with spice drawers, 5ft., c.1860's. £350-425

A pitch pine chiffonier, with seven drawers and shaped back, 6ft. 10in. wide, 4ft. 7in. high, c.1870. £450-500 LRG

51

Chests of Drawers

The chest of drawers as we know it grew out of the coffer. During the sixteenth century, on the Continent, it became fashionable to build a drawer or two into the base of a lidded coffer or chest. These pieces of furniture are often called mule chests. The British cabinet-makers soon followed the trend and produced the first true chests of drawers.

By the seventeenth century the chests of drawers had become established as an essential piece of furniture. By the end of the century the chest of drawers had appeared in a form not materially different from that produced today. Pine was used firstly as a carcase to be veneered by 'superior' woods and secondly, as the staple chest for attics, staff, nursery accommodation; and farmhouse and cottage furniture.

There is a wide range of pine chests to be found; from the plain purely functional type to the highly decorated and ornately carved example. Some chests were originally painted and should this remain these should *not* be stripped. Even more examples have been recently painted and have a market quite distinct from the collector of pine in its natural state.

A Georgian pine chest of five long and two short drawers, on original bracket feet, 57in. high, 43in. wide. £275-325 RC

A pine chest of drawers, on bracket feet, 3ft. 8in. high, 3ft. 4in. wide, c.1830. £150-200 AL

A Regency part bedroom suite, in original scumble to simulate birds eye maple and lined oak, c.1815.
Dressing table: £200-250
Wash-stand: £185-200 *SW*

A Victorian pine chest of drawers, 3ft. wide. £90-110

A pine Biedermeier chest, 33in. high, 42in. wide, 21in. deep, c.1830. £200-250 Sca

An early 18th C. pine batchelor's chest, with fold-over top, originally veneered in walnut, 36in. high, 42in. wide. £1,100-1,200 Jos

A Georgian pine chest of drawers, on bracket feet, 3ft. 2in. high, 3ft. 3in. wide, 22in. deep c.1790. £240-375 PH

A Victorian pine chest of drawers, with shaped base and beech handles, 37in. high, 35in. wide, 17in. deep. £125-145 AH

A Georgian pine chest of drawers, on bracket feet, 37in. high, 34in. wide, 21in. deep. £210-250 PJ

A Georgian pine chest of drawers, on bracket feet, c.1810. £120-140 RK

An early pine chest of drawers, with original knobs and wooden escutcheons, 36in. wide, c.1780. £120-140 AL

A pine chest of drawers, on new shaped base, 32in. wide. £75-110 WH

A pine chest of drawers, cock beaded drawers, full dust liners, original feet and knobs, 3ft. high, 4ft. wide, 18in. deep, c.1780. £185-250 SW

A Georgian pine serpentine chest, with bracket feet, 30in. high, 36in. wide. £800-900 Jos

A Regency pine chest of drawers, with original handles, 33in. wide, c.1835. £160-180 AL

A mid 19th C. pine chest of drawers, with carved supports, with four drawers, 2ft. 10in. high, 3ft. 9in. wide. £220-240 MV

A Victorian pine splashback chest, with shaped back, 39in. wide, c.1840. £130-160 W

An early 19th C. pine chest, 40in. high, 32in. wide, 19in. deep. £195-250 Bed

A mid-Victorian pine chest of drawers, 3ft. high, 4ft. wide, 18in. deep, c.1860. £90-135 SW

A Scandinavian painted pine chest of drawers, 3ft. high, 3ft. 1in. wide. £120-140 BEL

A pine chest, on turned feet, 45in. high, 40in. wide, 22in. deep. £100-150 PJ

A small late-Victorian pine chest, with glass crystal handles, standing on turned feet, 32in. high, 43in. wide, 19in. deep. £100-150 PJ

A pine chest of drawers, 33in. high, 34in. wide, 18in. deep, c.1860 £100-120 AL

A low pine chest of drawers, 41in. wide, c.1860. £85-125 W

A Victorian pine chest of drawers, with beech handles, 50in. high, 36in. wide, 11in. deep. £120-145 AH

A pine chest, with secret drawer, spring catch revealed when top right hand drawer is removed, with ivory escutcheons, c.1850. £200-250 Sca

An English pine chest of drawers, 34in. high, 25in. wide, 18½in. deep, c.1840. £100-150 WH

A Victorian pine chest of drawers, with beech handles and turned feet, 34in. high, 36in. wide, 17in. deep. £110-130 AH

A pine bow-fronted chest of drawers, with mahogany edging, 43in. high, 36in. wide, 19in. deep, c.1870. £150-200 WH The mahogany veneer has been removed to reveal well made pine carcass.

A gallery-back pine chest of drawers, with porcelain handles, 38in high, 40in. wide, 20in. deep, c.1880. £150-175 PF

A pitch pine chest of drawers, 49in. high, 42in. wide, 20in. deep. £150-200 PJ

A Scandinavian painted pine chest of drawers, recently painted, 3ft. 1in. high, 3ft. 2in. wide, c.1890. £140-160 BEL

A Welsh pine chest, with carved decoration, 50in. high, 43½in. wide, 22in. deep, c.1860. £150-200 WH

An early Victorian pine five drawer chest, with applied split turnings, 36in. high, 42in. wide, 20in. deep. £190-250 CRA

A German pine chest, 35½in. high, 41in. wide, 23½in. deep, c.1840. £250-300 Sca

A pine chest of drawers, two short and two long drawers, 34in. high, 41½in. wide, 17in. deep, c.1860. £85-110 HH

A Danish pine chest, with carved and reeded columns and moulded drawers, on bun feet, 37in. high, 36in. wide, 21in. deep. £280-320   Bed

A small Victorian pine chest, with brass handles, 32½in. high, 25in. wide, 16in. deep, c.1860. £300-350   W

A late-Victorian pine chest of drawers, with replacement handles, 36in. high, 36in. wide, 18in. deep. £150-200   Sw

A pine chest of drawers, with split turned decoration. £100-150   DPN

A late 19th C. pine chest of drawers, with moulded drawers, split turned decorations to sides, 31in. high, 39in. wide. £150-200   Ad

A pine chest of drawers, 38in. wide, c.1890. £95-150   W

A 19th C. pine chest of drawers, 41in. high, 40in. wide. £100-135   Ad

A late 19th C. Austrian pine chest of drawers, 34in. high, 41in. wide. £190-230   Ad

A 19th C. pine chest of drawers, with original porcelain handles, 32in. high, 34in. wide, 18in. deep. £85-120   GLF

A 19th C. pine chest of drawers, 41in. high, 42in. wide, 22in. deep. £80-120   GLF

A 19th C. painted pine chest, 48½in. high, 40in. wide. £200-250   Ad

A decorative painted pine chest of drawers, 40in. high, 40in. wide. £175-200   PF

An Edwardian pine chest, with original brass handles, on turned feet, 43in. high, 36in. wide, 19in. deep. £120-160   PJ

A decorative painted pine chest of drawers, 42in. high, 38in. wide, 18in. deep. £175-200   PF

A decorative painted pine chest of drawers, 30in. high, 42in. wide, 21in. deep. £175-200   PF

An Edwardian pine chest of drawers, with original brass handles, on bracket feet, 34in. wide. £110-140   Co

An Art Nouveau pine chest of drawers, with original brass handles, 35in. high, 30in. wide. £120-140   MV

A decorative painted pine chest of drawers, 42in. high, 38in. wide, 18in. deep. £175-200   PF

A Scandinavian pine chest of drawers, 91in. high, 100in. wide. £110-145   BEL

A decorative painted pine chest of drawers, 36in. high, 38in. wide, 19in. deep. £175-200 PF

A small pine dressing chest, with original handles, and shaped back and shelf, sound condition throughout, c.1820. £130-150 Sw

A decorative painted pine chest of drawers, 42in. high, 38in. wide, 18in. deep. £175-200 PF

A Danish pine tallboy, with applied split turnings, 72in. high, 36in. wide, 24in. deep, c.1865. £320-380 Bed

A Scottish pine chest of drawers, with one deep top drawer, made to appear as five small drawers, 3ft. 10in. high, 3ft. 8in. wide. £180-200 PF

A late 19th C. serpentine fronted chest of drawers, with splashback and applied split turnings, 48in. high, 39in. wide. £150-200 PF

A decorative painted pine chest of drawers, 40in. high, 40in. wide, 20in. deep. £175-200 PF

An Irish pine chest of drawers, with splashback, on turned feet, c.1880. £85-100 RK

A mid Victorian pine chest of drawers, with pot space, 34in. wide, c.1860. £125-175 W

Flights of Drawers

Pine was found to be the perfect material for small pieces of utilitarian furniture, such as flights of drawers. These pieces can well be regarded as among the most collectable pine pieces. They are small, can fit into most homes and are on the whole attractive.

It is true to say of most pine that if it is functional, decorative and not too large it will be at a premium. One must stress again that condition and colour are also very important when assessing the value of a pine piece.

Flights of drawers were originally made as spice drawers for domestic use, or as storage drawers for shops and workshops. Many of the spice drawers can still be found with their original paintwork, especially painted labels. These add considerably to the value of the piece, and should not be removed.

A 19th C. pine set of spice drawers, 8in. wide, 6in. high. £35-45

A small pine chest of drawers, 1ft. 6in. wide, c.1880. £35-45 AL

A Victorian pine specimen chest, with original handles, 2ft. 6in. high. £90-100 AL

A 19th C. pine set of spice drawers, 10in. high, 6in. wide. £35-40

A pine flight of drawers, with original handles, 2ft. 8in. by 9in. by 10in., c.1850. £75-100 AL

A Victorian pine spice cabinet, with fifteen various sized drawers with brass handles, damaged, woodworm in back, 7½ by 18 by 28in. £85-100 AL

A pine nest of drawers, 2ft. high, 4ft. 7in. wide, 11in. deep, c.1850. £225-250 PH

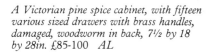

An early 19th C. small pine chest of drawers, with original handles, 12 by 9 by 5½in. £40-50 AL

A flight of pine grocery drawers, 2ft. 7in. high, 4ft. 2in. wide, c.1890. £375-425 BEL

A pine flight of drawers, 5ft. 3in. high, 2ft. wide, 1ft. 8in. deep, c.1840. £150-175 MB

A pine specimen cabinet, each drawer having plate glass top and desiccant container fitted, 20 by 14 by 30in., c.1890. £175-200 Bed

An 18th C. pine spice cabinet, with oak drawers, 16 by 14½in. £80-85 AL

A 19th C. pine miniature chest of drawers, with small brass handles, 16in. wide, 15in. high. £55-65

A small 19th C. pitch pine specimen cabinet, with iron carrying handle, 11in. high, 14in. wide. £55-65

A 19th C. pine flight of cobblers drawers, with original mahogany handles, 21in. high, 25in. wide, 10in. deep. £90-95 AL

A late Victorian pine collectors cabinet, with graduated drawers and compartment, painting of birds of top, 18in. high, 15in. wide, 8in. deep. £100-125 W

A Victorian pine specimen chest, with seven graduated drawers, 34in. wide. £150-200

A small pine specimen chest, 15 by 14 by 12in. £35-45 AL

Dressing Chests

Dressing chests have been an essential piece of furniture since early in the eighteenth century. The term was coined by Chippendale and re-defined by Sheraton as meaning 'a small case of drawers, containing four drawers in height, the uppermost of which is divided into conveniences for dressing'.

At this time the dressing chest looked like any other chest of drawers – except that the top drawer was divided into small compartments usually centred by a hinged mirror which would be raised for use or laid flat to allow the drawer to close.

Later it became more common to place a swivel mirror on top of an ordinary chest of drawers. This mirror was frequently placed on top of two small drawers. This is the most common form of the dressing chest, or dressing table, to be found in pine in the nineteenth century. Dressing tables are always in demand and decorative examples of a good colour have always commanded good prices. This is an area where a judicious buy of a painted dressing table at a local house sale can provide a piece with potential. Check that the dressing table is pine by scraping off some paint in an inconspicuous spot. The auctioneer may not be too delighted by this! If you buy it – do start to strip the top first as it's heart-breaking to spend hours stripping the chest only to find there is a ghastly stain on the surface.

A pine dressing table, with original handles, 38in. wide, 57in. high, 20in. deep, c.1860. £170-180   AL

A 19th C. pine dressing table, with swing mirror, turned legs, 58in. high, 30in. wide, 17in. deep. £75-125   PCo

A pine dressing chest, with replacement handles, 33in. wide, 60in. high, 18in. deep c.1900. £130-140   AL

A Victorian pine dressing table, 5ft. 4in.
high, *20½in. deep, 42in. wide, c.1860.*
£125-150   HH

A pine dressing chest, 37in. wide.
£100-200   WH

A pine dressing table, 65in. high, 39in.
wide, 20in. deep, c.1870. £225-250   W

An Edwardian dressing chest, with
original brass handles and bevelled mirror.
£150-200   PJ

A late Victorian pine dressing chest, with
original brass handles, 60in. high, 36in.
wide, 20in. deep. £130-150   Sw

A pine dressing table, 67in. high, 42in.
wide, 19in. deep, c.1890. £225-250   W

A Scandinavian pine dressing chest, with
mirror, drawer and cupboard, 78in. high,
32in. wide. £150-175   BEL

A late Victorian pitch pine dressing table,
66in. high, 45in. wide, 18in. deep.
£150-175   PJ

Washstands

Washstands have undergone a large number of changes in style. The earliest examples tended to be rather elaborate contrivances, sometimes with their own water cisterns, taps and plug holes which allowed used water to drain into a bucket or bowl placed underneath for emptying by a servant. These pieces were certainly for use by the master and mistress of the house.

As time passed and a more developed plumbing system appeared – allowing actual running water into the nation's master bedrooms, washstands became simpler and plainer. These were very much for use by the lesser members of the household. These washstands can have plain tops or a top centred by a jug and basin set. Some have quite decorative tiled backs; especially desirable are those with Art Nouveau tiles. These are much in demand by interior designers as interesting additions to the bathroom décor – often finished off by the inevitable green fern!

A Georgian pine washstand, 29in. high, 14in. wide, 14in. deep. £115-130

A Regency pine washstand, 3ft. 9in. high by 2ft. 2in. deep, c.1840. £100-130   AL

A 19th C. pine corner washstand, with a shaped base, 2ft. 6in. wide, 3ft. 2in. high. £40-50

A Georgian pine washstand/pot cupboard, originally painted mahogany, 38in. high, 15in. square. £400-450   Jos

A late Georgian pine washstand 16in. wide. £75-110

An unusual pine washstand, 35in. wide by 38in. high, c.1820. £100-125   AL

A Regency pine washstand, of ten drawers, central cupboard, fitted bowl, marble top, 3ft. 2in. high, 3ft. wide. £150-180   *MV*

A 19th C. pine washstand, with high back, two drawers, shaped frieze and turned legs, with side stretchers, 36in. wide, 39in. high, 20in. deep. £60-65

A Regency pine washstand, 38in. high, 22in. wide, 15½in. deep. £150-170   *W*

A pair of pine washstands, 3ft. wide, c.1825. £160-190   *AL*

A double pine washstand, 39in. wide, 35in. high, 19in. deep, c.1840. £60-70   *AL*

A small 19th C. pine washstand, with scalloped back and sides, turned legs and drawer to base, 24in. wide, 34in. high, 15in. deep. £35-40

A pine washstand, 36in. wide, c.1880. £90-120

A Victorian pine washstand, 34in. wide. £70-80   *Co*

A gallery-back pine washstand, 35in. high, 25in. wide, 18in. deep. £75-95   *PF*

A pine washstand, 36in. high, 33in. wide, 18in. deep, c.1820. £75-100   *WH*

A 19th c. pine washstand, with bamboo legs and one drawer, 37in. high, 33in. wide, 19in. deep. £90-120   *AH*

A Victorian pine semi-circular washstand, with carved legs and shaped back, 38in. high, 36in. wide, 18in. deep. £95-110   *AH*

A pine cupboard/washstand, with marble top, 3ft. by 1ft. 10in. by 2ft. 7in. high, c.1880. £190-220 PCA

A Victorian lyre-ended pine washstand, with two drawers and shaped base, 38in. wide, 48in. high. £110-120

An early 20th C. pine washstand, with shaped back, towel rails and base drawer, 38in. high, 34in. wide, 17in. deep. £95-115 AH

A Victorian pine washstand, 36in. wide. £75-85 Co

An early 19th C. pine washstand, with shaped back-board, 36in. high, 42in. wide, 18in. deep. £60-75 DPN

A Victorian pine washstand/bedside table, 9in. wide. £55-85

A 19th C. pine washstand, with turned legs and shaped back board and base, 18in. deep, 3ft. high, 3ft. wide. £55-65

A pine washstand, with base drawer, 23in. wide, c.1860 £60-90 W

A late Victorian pine washstand, 2ft. 10in. high, 2ft. 5in. wide, 1ft. 8in. deep. £80-90 PCA

A 19th C. pine washstand, 37in. high, 20in. wide. £40-60 GLF

A Victorian pine washstand, 24in. wide.
£60-80

An Irish pine washstand, with shaped
superstructure and small single drawer.
30in. high, 42in. wide, 22in. deep.
£75-95   HH

A pine washstand, 31in. wide, c.1890.
£55-75   W

A marble topped pine washstand, 36in.
wide. £90-150   WH

A Swedish pine washstand/side cabinet,
32½in. wide c.1890. £160-185   Far

A satin walnut washstand, with turned
legs, marble back with small mirror, single
cupboard below, with brass handles, 62in.
high, 42in. wide, 20in. deep.
£125-150   PJ

A 19th C. pine washstand, with one
drawer, 3ft. wide, 30in. high, 19in. deep.
£60-70

A pine washstand, 37in. high.
£60-80   WH

A pine washstand, 31in. wide, c.1900.
£55-70   Ad

A Victorian pine washstand, with marble
top, pink tiled splashback, 36in. £85-125

A pine washstand, 35in. wide, c.1850.
£120-145   W

A late Victorian pine washstand, with marble top and tiled splashback. £85-125

A pine washstand, with original brass handles, 29in. wide, 46in. high, 17in. deep, c.1860. £110-120   AL

A pine washstand, 45in. high, 42in. wide, 20in. deep, c.1860. £125-175   W

A late Victorian pine marble-topped washstand, 36in. wide. £120-150

An Art Nouveau pine washstand, with original tiles and handles, black marble top. £90-120   D

A pine washstand, 44in. high, 34in. wide, 17in deep, c.1850. £75-125   WH

A German pine washstand, 30½in. high, 33½in. wide, 20½in. deep, c.1900. £200-250   Sca

A pair of pine washstands, 3ft. 2in. high, 3ft. 2in. wide, 1ft. 7in. deep. £150-175   CRP

A Victorian pine marble topped washstand, with two drawers, fretwork sides and shaped centre stretcher, 38in. high, 48in. wide. £90-120

Beds and Cradles

The first beds to be introduced were particularly uncomfortable pieces of furniture. Due to the universal belief that the night air was filled with noxious vapours and also due to houses beset by draughts; the four-poster was developed. These were fitted with all-enclosing drapes to protect the upper classes.

A pine bed, furnished with Laura Ashley prints, in 19th C. style. Complete £1,000-1,200 Jos

Many of the poorer people slept in almost coffin-shaped cupboards built into wall-recesses, with wooden doors that could be pulled shut to keep out the poisonous air and doubtless, goblins, werewolves and other denizens of the night. The fact that so many people slept in these beds and lice, bed-bugs, (to say nothing of numerous diseases) were rampant – things must have been quite unpleasant!

At this time – the moneyed classes insisted that all attention was lavished on the exterior structure. It was left to the Victorians to develop interior springing and also to extend the size of the beds. A warning note for those intent on buying an *original* bed – it will be *short*.

The pine beds shown here tend to come from the Victorian period and the most desirable frequently come from Scandinavia.

A note here about reproduction pine – there are some excellent firms making new beds from old pine. In most cases these can be more practical as they are made to a size to take a modern mattress. Many pine dealers will also arrange for a period bed to be extended to the 'right' size.

A Victorian Welsh pine double bed. £275-325   Co

A 20th C. Swedish pine bed settle, with shaped back rails, 2ft. 9in. high, 6ft. long, 22in. wide. £250-300

A Swedish pine box bed, with finials and turned arms, 3ft. 8in. high, 6ft. 4in. long, 22in. wide, c.1850-80. £300-400   CC

A Victorian style pine rocking crib, 33in. long, 22in. high, 19in. wide. £90-130 PF

A Scandinavian pine extending bed, in three sections, opening to 6ft. long, c.1800. £300-350 W

An early 19th C. pine rocking cradle. £100-125 COR

A pine hooded cradle, 27in. high, 3ft. 3in. long, 17in. wide, c.1750. £125-150 HH

A pine cradle, with hood, in mid 19th C. style. £150-180 Mv

A Scandinavian carved pine bed, 74in. long. £135-185

A Danish pine bed, 76in. long. £135-185

A Swedish pine settle bed, 6ft. by 1ft. 9in., c.1880. £260-295 PCA

A German pine bed, 75in. long, 37in. wide, 51in. high, c.1890. £75-100 WH

A pine cradle, 2ft. 9in. by 1ft. 4in., c.1840. £150-175 PCA

A mid 19th C. carved pine single bed, 36in. wide. £175-200 PF

A pine bed, (head only shown,) with original sides and slats, 4ft. 6in. wide, c.1840. £200-250 AL

Armoires and Wardrobes

In mediaeval times the nobility stored their finest garments in the castle 'garde-robes' for safe-keeping. This may not immediately strike the modern reader as remarkable until it is pointed out that the garde-robe was another name for a small indoor privy built into the castle wall and lacking the benefit of running water. This extremely unpleasant atmosphere was the first known moth-repellant!

From such unsavoury beginnings grew the wardrobe. It was soon to become an essential piece of bedroom furniture. In the sixteenth and seventeenth centuries clothes were normally stored folded flat in chests and presses. It was not until the eighteenth century that free-standing wardrobes became popular. These took over very quickly and within a short time there were a great many styles available; from the vast breakfront, architectural types to quite simple pieces. These, in pine, fit ideally into today's taste in bedroom furniture; the most popular being the Scandinavian pieces and the small decorative ladies' wardrobe with a mirror front.

A cautionary note: – do measure carefully before you purchase a large wardrobe. Is the room tall enough? Can you get it round that bend in the stair? Many a man-hour has been spent attempting the impossible with an over-sized wardrobe or cupboard!

An early Victorian pine gentleman's press, 3ft. wide. £250-300

A Georgian pine press, with arched fielded panels, 6ft. 10in. 3ft. 10in. wide, 1ft. 11in. deep, c.1760. £500-600   PH

A Georgian pine press, 5ft. 9in. high, 4ft. 4in. wide, 22in. deep, c.1760. £450-550   PH

A Georgian pine Welsh linen press, 73in. high, 42in. wide. £420-480   Co

An Irish pine press, 58in. wide, c.1790. £650-750   Ad

An Irish pine panelled cupboard, with four doors, c.1780. £650-700   PH

A Scottish pine press cupboard, 6ft. 2in. high, 4ft. 4in. wide, 21in. deep, c.1800. £450-550   PH

A Georgian pine linen press, with slides, 92in. high, 53in. wide, 23in. deep. £300-400   DPN

A 19th C. pine linen press, 85in. high, 74in. wide. £300-350   Ad

An 18th C. pine linen press, with ornate carving, 78in. high, 56in. wide. £400-500   Ad

A pine press, with panelled sides, 6ft. 8in. high, 3ft. 8in. wide, 19in. deep, c.1840. £375-425   PH

A good Regency pine linen press, with porcelain knobs, all original, 6ft. 5in. high, 4ft. wide, 18in. deep, c.1815. £400-485   SW

A small Victorian pine linen press, with shelves, 70in. high, 40in. wide. £350-400   AL

A pine linen press, with slides, in two sections, 60in. wide, c.1860. £380-420   AL

An 18th C. Welsh pine Chippendale style linen press, with blind fret top, reeded and canted corners and geometric moulded panels, the dropped well at base of cupboard with four false drawers, and five drawers below, peg joined and standing on bracket feet, 6ft. high, 4ft. wide. £650-750

A pine gentleman's wardrobe, on cabriole lgs, 6ft. high, 47in. wide, 23½in. deep, c.1830. £550-650   HH

A 19th C. pine linen press, with five drawers, 77in. high, 41in. wide, 20in. deep. £300-400

A French pine armoire, 7ft. 4in. high, 5ft. wide, 21½in. deep, c.1850. £350-400   HH

An early Victorian pine double wardrobe, with carved columns, 80in. high, 44in. wide, 20in. deep. £375-425   PF

An exceptional Georgian pine gentleman's wardrobe, in good original order, 7ft. 6in. high, 4ft. 6in. wide, 18in. deep. £485-600   SW

A finely panelled Scottish pine hanging cupboard, 6ft. 1in. high, 4ft. 6in. wide, c.1800. £350-400   HG

A pine wardrobe, possibly Hungarian, 78in. high, 54in. wide, 26in. deep. c.1800. £900-1,000   Sca

A Victorian pine wardrobe, 72in. high. £150-175   Co

A late 19th C. Dutch pine wardrobe, with panelled doors, 6ft. 6in. high, 3ft. 10in. wide. £325-375   BEL

A 19th C. Continental pine armoire, in the style of a faux secretaire, with decorative panels and carved pediment, 6ft. high, 3ft. wide. £375-400   DH

A 19th C. Continental pine armoire, the single door with raised fielded panels, 6ft. high, 2ft. 9 in. wide. £210-250   DH

A 19th C. Continental pine armoire, with arcaded panels to the doors, 6ft. 4in. high, 3ft. 2in. wide. £350-400   DH

A Scandinavian pine wardrobe, 184cm. high, 94cm. wide. £140-180   BEL

A 19th C. pine wardrobe and washstand, with two drawers and cupboard with panelled doors, 77in. high, 43in. wide, 18in. deep. £300-350   AL

A French pine marriage armoire, with panelled doors, well carved, 7ft. 3in. high, 4ft. 2in. wide, 19in. deep, c.1840. £1,100-1,400   PH

A 19th C. pine linen cupboard, 78in. high, 41in. wide. £175-225   GLF

An Irish pine cupboard, 7ft. high, 4ft. wide, c.1840. £240-270   RK

An Austrian pine wardrobe, 76in. high, 77in. wide, 27in. deep, c.1730. £1,400-1,600   Sca

A 19th C. Scandinavian seven piece pine wardrobe, with panelled doors, with one drawer in base and standing on bun feet, 6ft. 4in. high, 3ft. 9in. wide, 21in. deep. £200-250

A large 19th C. pitch pine wardrobe, inset reeded moulding to either side of the door, 82in. high, 49in. wide, 22in. deep. £175-200

A 19th C. small pine wardrobe, recently painted with fairy designs, 5ft. high, 3ft. wide, 19in. deep. £225-250

A Victorian pine wardrobe, in eight sections, with original mirror, 78in. high, 58in. wide, 20in. deep, c.1860. £420-460   AL

A pine three section wardrobe, 83in. high, 70in. wide, 21½in. deep, c.1880. £600-650   W

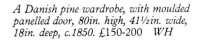

A Danish pine wardrobe, with moulded panelled door, 80in. high, 41½in. wide, 18in. deep, c.1850. £150-200   WH

A large 19th C. pine wardrobe, 74in. high, 60in. wide, 25in. deep. £400-450

A German pine armoire, 79in. high, 71in. wide, 28½in. deep, c.1850. £650-850   Sca

A very fine mid Victorian hall wardrobe, good oak scumble on pine, breaks to form six units, 6ft. 3in. high, 5ft. 8in. wide, 18in. deep, c.1860. £425-450   SW

A 19th C. Scandinavian pine wardrobe, with two fielded panelled doors, interior fitted with swivel pegs and a drop well in the base, 6ft. 7in. high, 3ft. 2in. wide, 17in. deep. £260-290

*A 19th C. Scandinavian pine wardrobe,
6ft. 4in. high, 2ft. 9in. wide.
£220-250   BEL*

*A pine wardrobe, 43in. wide, 78in. high,
21in. deep. £210-220   AL*

*A small pine wardrobe, 5ft. 8in. high, 3ft.
1in. wide. £180-220   BEL*

*A German painted pine armoire, dated
1881.* £400-500   WH

*A large pine wardrobe, with panelled
doors, in eight pieces, 7ft. 2in. high, 5ft.
4in. wide. £450-500   BEL*

*A Danish pine two door wardrobe, 69in.
high, 49in. wide, 19in. deep, c.1870.
£300-350   Bed*

*A large pine wardrobe, with panelled
doors, in seven pieces, 6ft. 8in. high, 5ft.
2in. wide. £350-400   BEL*

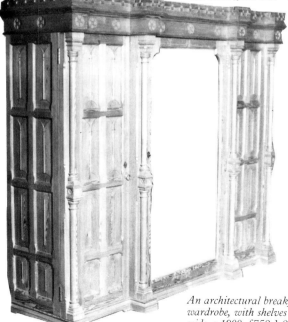

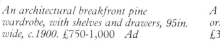

*An architectural breakfront pine
wardrobe, with shelves and drawers, 95in.
wide, c.1900. £750-1,000   Ad*

*A Danish pine breakdown wardrobe, all
original fittings, 77in. high, c.1870.
£300-375   W*

A Danish pine armoire, 6ft. 6in. high, 3ft. 6in. wide, c.1840. £150-200 RK
This cupboard actually has one door with a drawer below, the mock top doors and drawers being purely decorative.

A pine wardrobe, with original brass handles, 73in. high, c.1920. £80-125 W

A pine food cupboard, with panelled doors and two drawers, 75in. high, 50in. wide. £595-650 AD

A 19th C. Austrian pine armoire, 72½in. high, 39½in. wide. £350-385 Ad

An Austrian pine armoire, 72½in. high, 39½in. wide. £350-385 Ad

A German painted pine armoire, with small drawer in base, on bun feet, 6ft. 4in. high, 4ft. 7in. wide, c.1840. £450-500 BEL

A 19th C. pine wardrobe, with panelled doors, drawer in base, applied split turnings. £300-375 Ad

A late 19th C. pine linen press, 72in. high, 37in. wide. £300-350 Ad

An Edwardian pitch pine wardrobe, with deep drawer to base and porcelain handles, 78in. high, 32in. wide. £100-125

Bookcases

The history of the development of bookcases is one with a slow start. Although Caxton introduced the printing press to Britain before 1477, books remained rare and valuable possessions for nearly two hundred years. During the sixteenth century books were locked away in libraries and, not infrequently, chained to their shelves for extra security. They were mainly owned by the aristocracy, seats of learning and religious houses.

It was not until the seventeenth century that books were sufficiently widely owned for furniture designers to recognise the potential market for free standing bookcases.

Originally veneered or painted to resemble mahogany or rosewood, early pine bookcases have all the style of the best furniture of their period. Many were fitted into libraries and then painted to match the décor of the room. These early pine bookcases now command high prices.

The later pine bookcases of the nineteenth century follow closely the styles of their mahogany counterparts. Some can be slightly ungainly and clumsily put together – but others show all the best design features of the period. Another cautionary note – ceiling heights have dropped considerably since these fine pieces were built. Make sure your room will take the height!

An Irish pine astragal glazed bookcase, in original condition, 6ft. 6in. high, 3ft. 9in. wide, c.1810. £550-600   RK

A Welsh pine breakfront bookcase, with replacement grills, 6ft. 6in. high, 7ft. 6in. wide, c.1800. £1,150-1,200   RK

A late Georgian pine breakfront bookcase, with adjustable shelves and drawers to base, 102in. high, 79in. wide. £2,000-2,500   RC

A Scottish pine breakfront bookcase, original throughout, 9ft. high, 14ft. wide, c.1820. £2,000-2,500   RK

A Welsh pine bookcase, 86in. high, 41in. wide, 23in. deep, c.1840.
£550-650   Sca

A Georgian style yellow pine bookcase, with dentil moulding and applied split turnings, 6ft. 6in. high, 3ft. wide.
£100-150   GHM

An Irish pine country bookcase, 6ft. 6in. high, 3ft. 6in. wide, c.1850.
£200-250   RK

An Irish pine glazed cupboard, on chest of drawers base, with rope twist mouldings, sunburst drawers and reeded doors.
£550-650   RC

A 19th C. pine collector's cabinet, with glazed top. £600-650   COR

An Irish pine country bookcase, 6ft. 6in. high, 3ft. 6in. wide, c.1850.
£200-250   RK

A Welsh pine display cabinet, 85in. high, 54in. wide, 19in. deep, c.1815.
£850-950   Sca

A Northern Irish pine bookcase, with Gothic arched doors, 6ft. 6in. high, 5ft. wide, c.1830. £350-400   RK

A pine secretaire bookcase, 77in. high, 39½in. wide, 21in. deep, c.1820.
£1,250-1,500   W

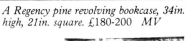
A Regency pine revolving bookcase, 34in. high, 21in. square. £180-200   MV

A pitch pine bookcase, 80in. high, 51in. wide, 16in. deep, c.1830. £300-400   WH

A pine bookcase, 75in. high, 45in. wide. £250-300   Ad

A Victorian pine bookcase, with original glass handles, 4ft. wide. £325-400

A Victorian pine bookcase, with astragal glazed doors and adjustable shelves. £750-850   RC

A Victorian revived Gothic-style stained pine breakfront bookcase, 8ft. 2in. high, 8ft. 10in. wide. £1,200-1,400   CDC

A small Victorian pine bookcase, 74in. high, 44in. wide, 16in. deep, c.1860. £280-320   AL

A Victorian bookcase/china cabinet, the two parts probably married, 50in. wide. £375-425

A pine glazed bookcase, 70in. high, 39in. wide, 13½in. deep, c.1850. £150-200   Sca

A Victorian pine bookcase, with carved moulding to top of glazed doors and cushion moulded drawers, 48in. wide. £350-400

A reproduction pine astragal breakfront bookcase, 81in. high, 77in. wide, 21in. deep. £900-1,000   PF

A pine glazed top bookcase, with three-quarter turned pillars to top and base, dentil moulding, and cushion moulded drawer fronts, 82in. high, 46in. wide, 14in. deep. £300-350 GHM

A Scottish pine open bookcase, 9ft. high, 5ft. 6in. wide, c.1870. £520-570 RK

An English pine farmhouse cupboard, 78in. high, 38in. wide, 19in. deep, c.1860. £220-280 WH

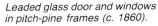
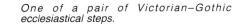

Chairs

Pine is not an ideal wood for use as a functional chair; beech, elm and yew having more strength. Manufacturers of chairs have always had to face one major problem – that of combining an attractive design with the strength required to withstand constant use.

The stresses placed upon chair backs and upon the joinery of seat and legs is truly enormous. This is particularly true if you allow your guests to rock on the back legs!

For this reason chairs should always be inspected most carefully before being bought for use. Some auctioneers hang chairs from the ceiling prior to an auction – it is well worth asking to see them at close quarters. Once the back joints have come apart they can rarely be repaired satisfactorily. Most vulnerable are those chairs whose two back uprights are jointed into the seats independently of the back legs.

Good sets of country chairs are now in great demand. There has been a tremendous increase in awareness of country pieces. It is often a sensible economic decision to buy country chairs singly and build your own harlequin set of kitchen chairs. This can be enormous fun and a single chair can often sell quite cheaply in a local auction.

An 18th C. Welsh commode chair, 50in. high. £750-800   Jos

An 18th C. English 'fool's' chair. £45-50

A slatback carver chair, c.1850. £80-120   PH

A Tiverton chair, in beech with elm seat, with contemporary tin repairs. £60-70   AL

An early 18th C. Welsh comb back chair. £350-400   Co

An early Windsor splat back single chair, in elm and ash, c.1780. £40-60   Sw

A set of six late Georgian ash ladder back chairs, two arm chairs and four singles, in original condition, c.1810.
£1,000-1,500 *Sw*

A pair of simulated bamboo chairs, 33in. high, 17½in. wide, 14in. deep, c.1840.
£100-125 *W*

A 19th C. child's Windsor chair.
£140-180 *Co*

An ash and fruitwood side chair, with box stretchers, rush seated, c.1780.
£80-100 *Sw*

An Irish 'fool's' chair, 30in. high, 18½in. wide, 11½in. deep. £80-100 *W*

A rare pair of Victorian pine hall chairs, c.1850. £120-150 *AL*

A Regency cane seat chair, 33in. high, 21in. wide, 17in. deep. £175-200 *W*

A cane seated chair and a rush seated chair, c.1860. £40-50 each *AL*

An elm splatback Windsor carver, c.1860.
£85-100 *SW*

An unusual carved pine rustic bench, the back and arms in the form of naturalistic branches carved with leaves and with a bear seated in the branches, the plank seat supported by standing carved bears, 4ft. 2½in. wide, probably Swiss, c.1860.
£1,800-2,200 *S*

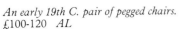

An early 19th C. pair of pegged chairs.
£100-120 *AL*

An elm and beech kitchen chair.
£35-40 WH

A set of three chairs, c.1850. £90-120 W

A set of eight chairs, the carvers converted
to rocking chairs, rockers, c.1840.
£800-850 W

A Victorian elm and beech country chair.
£75-100

A 20th C. Windsor chair. £30-35 AL

An 18th C. Spanish chestnut country
chair. £30-40 DH

A scroll back kitchen chair. £25-30 AL

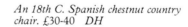

An elm and beech kitchen chair.
£20-25 WH

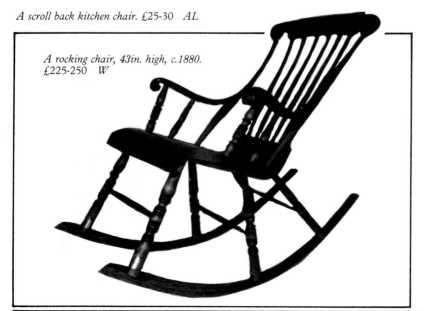

A rocking chair, 43in. high, c.1880.
£225-250 W

A set of four smokers' chairs, 31½in.
high, c.1860. £500-550 W

An Arts and Crafts hall chair, 30in. high.
£150-200   W

A child's Victorian high/rocking chair.
£125-145   PF

An unusual early 19th C. pine and beech
child's chair. £35-50   COR

An unusual smokers' bow chair, c.1850.
£100-150   PH

A high chair, 40in. high, c.1850.
£60-80   AL

A chapel pew, 36in. high, 66in. wide,
15in. deep. £75-100   Bed

A 19th C. pine and oak Irish rocking
chair, 39in. high. £70-95   PCo

A wheel-back carver, c.1880.
£120-140   PF

Clocks

Pine clock cases have been made since the eighteenth century but became much more popular in the nineteenth century. They were basically copies of the finer examples made in mahogany. Their main attraction is in the mellow honey colour as compared to their much darker mahogany and oak equivalents.

The best examples are either the plain moulded early eighteenth century examples or the carved and decorated nineteenth century clocks.

Many pine clock cases have been cut down as the plinth is particularly susceptible to rot. This should decrease the price asked. Colour is once again one of the major value points. Wax polish can make a tremendous difference to the appearance of pine. A badly stripped piece, which has not been neutralised properly will never attain the 'honey' colour so sought after.

A 19th C. pine longcase clock, 82in. high. £350-400 Co

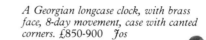

A Georgian longcase clock, with brass face, 8-day movement, case with canted corners. £850-900 Jos

A pine 8-day longcase clock, 6ft. 8in. high, c.1820. £500-550 MV

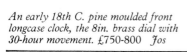

An early 18th C. pine moulded front longcase clock, the 8in. brass dial with 30-hour movement. £750-800 Jos

A pine 30-hour longcase clock, by Oldis of Dorchester, 6ft. 6in. high, 16in. wide, c.1760-1780. £420-450 MV

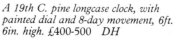

A 19th C. pine longcase clock, with painted dial and 8-day movement, 6ft. 6in. high. £400-500 DH

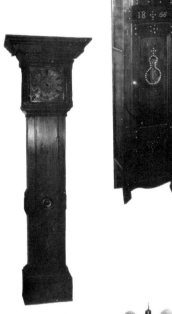

A French pine longcase clock, 6ft. 1in. high. £550-600   GF

A pine country-made clock, with bulls eye brass 30-hour single hand movement, originally 7ft. high but now reduced at the base. £650-700   Jos

A North of Ireland pine longcase clock, with moonphase arch dial, painted, and calendar, 214cm. high. £550-650   SAL

Commodes

A pine tray top commode, 31in. high, 19in. wide, 16½in. deep, c.1840. £250-300   W

A pine commode, 25in. wide. £75-100   WH

A pine step commode, with new leather, 20in. square, c.1850. £60-70   AL

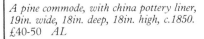

A pine commode, with china pottery liner, 19in. wide, 18in. deep, 18in. high, c.1850. £40-50   AL

An early Victorian pine step commode, 26in. high, 18in. wide, 30in. deep. £250-275   W

Boxes and Coffers

There has always been some confusion as to whether this utilitarian piece of furniture should be known as a coffer or a chest. Authorities today maintain that they should actually be called chests as they are not covered in leather.

This is not a new problem. According to the seventeenth century authority Randle Home, 'A coffer, if it have a straight and flat cover, is called a chest; which in all other things represents the coffer, save the want of a circular lid or cover'. The ancient craft of coffering having died of natural causes, no such distinction is made nowadays, and the two terms are largely interchangeable.

These coffers were primarily used as storage boxes intended for the safe-keeping of clothes and valuables. They represent man's earliest endeavours in the field of furnishings and fittings. Individual needs, taste and social standing have influenced size, style, quality and degree of decoration.

The examples shown here, being of pine, are among the most utilitarian of their kind. A good strong, robust example is greatly sought after; as extra storage space, coffee table or children's toy box.

An iron bound pine box, with secret front enclosing 21 graduated drawers, c.1810. £300-400 SAL

An early 18th C. pine deed box, date on exterior added later, three earlier dates inside, original iron handles and spearhead hinges, with pegged sides to lid. £100-125 PF

An 18th C. pitch pine coffer, 48in. wide, 25in. high, 18in. deep. £150-175

A Scandinavian pine dome top coffer, all original iron, c.1800. £145-200 W

A German painted pine chest, 45in., c.1850. £75-100 WH

A pine blanket chest, 3ft. wide, 2ft. high, 1ft. 7in. deep. £60-60 CRP

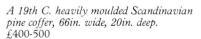

A 19th C. heavily moulded Scandinavian pine coffer, 66in. wide, 20in. deep. £400-500

A Welsh pine blanket chest, 47 by 19 by 17in. £120-150   Bed

A pine domed top box, with iron straps, 41in. wide, 19in. high, 18in. deep, c.1840. £65-80   AL

A pine dome top box, 23in. high, 45in. wide, 20in. deep, c.1840. £170-200   W

A Victorian pine coffer, with bracket feet and candle box, 41in. wide, 18in. high, 17in. deep. £70-80   AH

A 19th C. pine tool box, the interior fitted with trays, 19in. high, 31in. wide, 15in. deep. £100-120

A small early 19th C. domed pine box, with iron handles and clasp, 20in. long, 12in. deep, 10in. high. £50-70

A mid 19th C. Swedish painted pine dome top box, 4ft. 1in. wide, 2ft. deep, 2ft. 4in. high. £270-300   PCA

A small German painted pine box, 24½in. wide. c.1850's. £55-75   WH

A German painted pine chest, 48in. wide, c.1852. £75-120   WH

A 19th C. pine tool box, 11in. high, 35in. wide. £30-50   GLF

A pine box, with original handles, 39in. wide, 21in. high, 24in. deep. £60-70   AL

An unusual pine chest, with divided top and original locks, 48in. wide, c.1820. £220-260   AL

A pine box, 25in. high, 50in. wide, 23in. deep. £60-80 GLF

A German painted pine dome top chest, 50in. wide dated 1829. £175-200 WH

A 19th C. pine coffer, with iron handles, 2ft. 6in. wide, 19in. deep, 18in. high. £50-60

A Victorian pine coffer, with candle box, original hinges and keys, 33in. wide, 15in. high, 16in. deep. £60-70 AH

A 19th C. pine box, 11in. high, 28in. wide, 16in. deep. £40-60 GLF

A 19th C. pitch pine coffer, with interior candle box, 19in. high, 36in. wide. £45-50

An early 19th C. pine dome top seaman's box, 42in. wide, 26in. deep, 26in. high. £160-180 PF

A 19th C. iron bound pine sea chest, with shelf, 3ft. 6in. long, 2ft. high. £80-120 AL

A pine box, with trim round base, 29in. wide, 12in. high, 16in. deep. £40-50 AL

A German painted pine domed chest, 31in. wide, c.1860. £55-75 WH

A 19th C. pine coffer, in good condition, with original hinges, 38in. wide, 19in. deep, 19in. high. £60-80

A 19th C. pine chest, 38in. wide. £60-70 WH

A pine ammunition box, 24in. wide, 10½in. high, 12in. deep, c.1860. £30-40 AL

A 17th C. carved and panelled pine mule chest, 48in. wide, 30in. high, 18in. deep. £300-325 PH

An 18th C. pine linen chest, 25in. high, 40in. wide, 19in. deep. £130-150 GLF

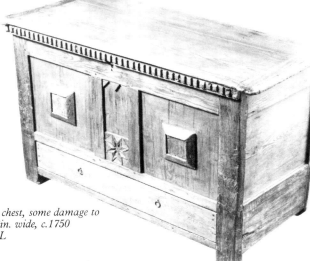

An early pine chest, some damage to mouldings, 46in. wide, c.1750 £130-160 AL

A pine chest, with well concealed secret drawers, replacement feet, 35in. wide, c.1860. £45-60 Far

A pine mule chest, with rising lid, 44 by 21 by 46in., c.1870. £200-250 Bed

A pine mule chest, with wooden hinges to lid, 39in. wide, c.1790. £95-150 W

A 19th C. pine mule chest, with hinged top and two drawers, 3ft. wide, 18in. deep, 2ft. 2in. high. £175-200

An Irish pine box over drawers, 4ft. wide, 3ft. 6in. high, 22in. deep, c.1800. £250-300 UP

An early 18th C. pine Bible box, with silhouette legs, 30in. high, 27in. wide. £600-650 Jos

A Georgian pine mule chest, 2ft. 4in. high, 1ft. 9½in. deep, 3ft. 4½in. wide. £110-130 CRP

A pine mule chest, 25in. high, 37in. wide, c.1830. £150-195   Ad

A pine coffer, 38 by 20 by 18in. £120-140   Bed

A 19th C. pine plank coffer, 20in. high, 47in. wide, 16in. deep. £140-170   CRA

A German pine trunk, 22½in. high, 40in. wide, 19¾in. deep, c.1800. £150-175   Sca

A mid 19th C. pine mule chest, with two drawers in base and shaped plinth, 44in. wide, 29in. high, 20in. deep. £150-175

A 19th C. pine mule chest, with rising lid, two drawers underneath, bracket feet, 40in. high, 40in. wide, 19in. deep. £180-225   PCo

Cupboards

As its name suggests, the cupboard was originally a board for cups. It was usually in the form of a table or shelves which would also be used for the display of plates.

Later, doors were added, either glazed or solid and since the sixteenth century the word cupboard has been accepted as the generic term for all items of furniture fitted with doors.

Pine corner cupboards are particularly in demand and good astragal glazed doors add considerably to the value of the piece.

A mid 19th C. pine desk/cupboard, 34in. wide. £120-180   WH

A pine cupboard, with panelled sides, 203 by 130 by 53cm., c.1780. £750-850   SAL

A North of Ireland pine bow-fronted corner cupboard, all original glass, 210cm. high, 100cm. wide. £850-950   SAL

A 19th C. pine cupboard, 34in. high, 20in. wide, 12in. deep. £40-80   GLF

A pine cupboard, with drawer, 27in. high, 22in. wide, 17½in. deep, c.1840. £30-40   AL

An 18th C. Irish pine food cupboard, with shaped and arcaded interior, fielded panelled doors and sides, 208 by 145 by 58cm. £750-850   SAL

An architectural pine corner cupboard, shaped interior originally a built-in piece, 214cm. high, 95cm. wide. £725-800   SAL

A 19th C. barrel-backed pine corner cupboard, with shaped shelves, 58in. high, 48in. wide, 20in. deep. £290-350   CRA

A pine two-door cupboard, 36½in. high, 33in. wide, 17½in. deep, c.1860. £90-110 AL

A deep pine two-door cupboard, 48in. high, 34in. wide, 22in. deep, c.1840. £110-120 AL

A late 19th C. small pine cupboard, with one drawer and two interior shelves, 30in. high, 30in. wide, 18in. deep. £75-100

A pine two-door cupboard, with adjustable shelves, 42in. high, 60in. wide, 13in. deep. £160-180 AL

A 19th C. Scandinavian pine cupboard, with fantail moulding to cupboard doors, 4ft. 6in. high, 2ft. 4in. wide, 18in. deep. £180-240

A 19th C. plain pine cupboard, with two shelves, 40in. high, 36in. wide, 16in. deep. £30-40

A 19th C. pine cupboard, with sliding doors and moulded panels, two shelves to interior, 59in. high, 62in. wide, 13in. deep. £160-170

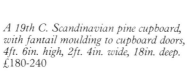

A small pine cupboard, 20in. high, 13in. wide, 11in. deep, c.1870. £25-35 AL

A 19th C. Continental pine cupboard, with two doors and one drawer, full columns on the corners, 3ft. high, 2ft. 4in. wide. £150-200 DH

A pine cupboard, 39½in. wide. £90-120 WH

A 19th C. small pine cupboard, standing on bun feet with one panelled door, 30in. high, 23in. wide, 16in. deep. £100-140

A pine gun cupboard, 67in. high, 38in. wide, c.1830. £85-100

A late 19th C. narrow pine cupboard, with panelled door, 59in. high, 25in. wide, 16in. deep. £80-100

A tall pine cupboard, with shaped door, shelf inside, 50in. high, 18in. wide, 13in. deep, c.1860. £110-130   AL

An early 18th C. pine gate-front food hutch, 28in. high, 27in. wide. £700-750   Jos

A Georgian Irish pine food cupboard, 6ft. 7in. high, 5ft. 6in. wide, 19in. deep, c.1780. £1,200-1,300   PH

A Georgian pine filing cabinet, 7ft. 6in. high, 54in. wide, c.1750. £300-350   AL

A Welsh pine shelved cupboard, 73in. high, 46in. wide, 14in. deep. £250-300   Bed

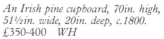

An Irish pine food cupboard, 7ft. high, 4ft. 6in. wide, c.1780. £1,400-1,800   UP

An Irish pine cupboard, 70in. high, 51½in. wide, 20in. deep, c.1800. £350-400   WH

An 18th C. French pine cupboard, with original hinges and two bottom drawers, 72in. high, 52in. wide. £750-1,000

An 18th C. Irish pine food cupboard, 79in. high, 63in. wide, 18in. deep. £590-650   Ad

An Irish pine cupboard, dentil cornice and reeded side columns, 7ft. high, 4ft. 6in. wide, 2ft. 6in. deep, c.1790. £500-550   MB

An Irish pine food cupboard, with good architectural interior, 84in. high, 57in wide. £850-1,000   RC

A pine blind bookcase, in the Adam style, in original condition except for later knobs, bow ended, the cornice is Greek key with egg and dart above, 8ft. 6in. high, 7ft. wide, c.1770. £1,800-2,200   RK

An Irish pine food cupboard, with fielded panel doors, 6ft. 8in. high, 4ft. 8in. wide, c.1800. £380-450   RK

An Irish pine cupboard, with a fine cornice with reeding below the arches, 7ft. high, 5ft. 5in. wide, c.1820. £450-500   RK

An 18th C. French pine cupboard, 5ft. 9in. high, 4ft. 8in. wide. £700-750   GF

An Irish pine cupboard, with fielded panels, 7ft. high, 4ft. 10in. wide, c.1800. £425-475   RK

An Irish pine cupboard, with unusual faceted panels to the doors, 7ft. high, 5ft. wide, c.1800. £425-495   RK

A 19th C. Irish pine food cupboard, 76in. high, 45in. wide, 18in. deep. £400-450   GLF

An Irish pine cupboard on cupboard, with interesting door design, 6ft. 5in. high, 4ft. 5in. wide, c.1790. £350-400 MB

An Irish pine tack cupboard, 6ft. 4in. high, 59in. wide, 17½in. deep, c.1800. £500-550   HH

A Scandinavian pine food cupboard, 187cm. high, 118cm. wide. £475-525   BEL

An Irish pine harness cupboard, with panelled doors, 6ft. 6in. high, 4ft. 6in. wide, c.1800. £350-450   MB

An Irish pine food cupboard, with knife drawer, 76½in. high, c.1820. £700-800   W

An Irish pine hall cupboard, 5ft. 10in. high, 49in. wide, 20in. deep, c.1820. £300-350   HH

A pine food cupboard, 50in. wide. £180-240   Far

An Irish pine food cupboard, with cats-eye moulding and arcaded and reeded interior surround, 7ft. high, 5ft. wide, 21in. deep, c.1840. £600-700

A home-made pine wall cupboard, with very old hinges, 40in. high, 27½in. wide, 9in. deep, c.1850. £60-80   WH

An English pine cupboard, with panelled doors, 41¾in. high, 40in. wide, 17in. deep, c.1840. £120-150   WH

An Irish pine food cupboard, with panelled doors and sides and fantail mouldings to cupboard doors, 6ft. 6in. high, 5ft. wide, 24in. deep, c.1850. £600-700

An Irish pine storage cupboard, 6ft. 6in. high, 5ft. 2in. wide, 12½in. deep, c.1840. £250-300   HH

A Welsh pine housekeeper's cupboard 7ft. 6in. high, 6ft. 3in. wide, 20in. deep c.1840. £800-£900   PH

An Irish pine cupboard, with fielded panels, bracket feet, 73in. high, 50in. wide, 18½in. deep, c.1780. £300-400   WH

An English pine bow-front corner cupboard, 42in. high, 30½in. wide, 17in. deep, c.1760. £200-250   WH

A Scottish pine food cupboard, 6ft. 6in. high, 4ft. wide, 21in. deep, c.1850. £500-600   PH

A German pine food cupboard, with frosted glass panels, 67in. high, 42in. wide, 20in. deep, c.1860. £260-300 WH

An Irish pine panelled food cupboard, 7ft. 2in. high, 5ft. 2in. wide, 19in. deep, c.1850. £600-700 PH

An Irish pine panelled cupboard, 6ft. 7in. high, 5ft. wide, 19in. deep, c.1850. £500-600 PH

A 19th C. pine kitchen cupboard, 48in. high, 8ft. wide, 12in. deep. £450-500 GLF

A Regency pine display cabinet, 86in. high, 49in. wide, 23in. deep. £2,200-2,600 W

A very good mid Victorian English pine housekeeper's cupboard; the base is standard, with seven drawers and a centre cupboard, with the desirable feature of two bread slides; the top has sliding doors between good turned and lozenged columns, c.1870. £450-500 SW

A pine kitchen press on a drawer base, 81in. high, 44in. wide, 21in. deep. £450-500 PF

A 19th C. Scandinavian pine cupboard with shelves, 45½in. wide. £250-300 Ad

An Irish pine bookcase, 6ft. 8in. high, 5in. wide, 17in. deep, c.1860. £325-375 HH

A Victorian pine pantry cupboard, 6ft. 3in. high. £375-475

A pine bookcase, 72in. high, 39in. wide, 14½in. deep, c.1880. £575-625   W

An early 18th C. pine glazed corner cupboard, with dentil cornice running into pediment, 6ft. 9in. high. £1,800-1,850   Jos

A Scandinavian pine corner cupboard, dated 1731, 72in. high. £395-450

An 18th C. pine corner cupboard, probably French, the grill front normally backed with material, 36in. wide, 56in. high. £600-800

An Irish pine astragal glazed corner cupboard, 7ft. 4in. high, 3ft. 4in. wide. £450-500   GF

A Scandinavian pine corner cupboard, with four doors, c.1760. £350-400   BEL

A Danish pine corner cupboard, 93in. high, 58½in. wide, 32½in. deep, c.1780. £850-950   WH

A fine 18th C. pine corner cupboard, in original condition, 7ft. 6in. high, c.1780. £850-900   RK

An 18th C. barrel back pine corner cupboard, with reeded side columns and dome, and three shaped shelves, 42in. wide, 60in. high. £700-750

An 18th C. pine corner cupboard, with reeded columns, dentil moulding and fielded panelled doors, 84in. high, 48in. wide. £900-1,000

An 18th C. barrel back pine corner cupboard, with gesso decoration to cupboard door, the dome carved out of a single piece of wood with dentil moulding to base, 84in. high, 42in. wide. £900-1,200

A mid 18th C. pine recess cupboard, with barrel back and domed interior, slide in waist, 6ft. 8in. high. £1,200-2,000 Jos

An 18th C. Irish pine corner cupboard, with rope twist and cottonreel mouldings, three drop drawers and shaped shelves to interior, 5ft. wide, 7ft. high, 27in. deep. £800-1,000

A Georgian pine full length bow front corner cupboard, 6ft. 8in. high. £1,900-2,000 Jos

An Irish pine corner cupboard, with fielded panels and drawer, 6ft. 3in. high, 3ft. 2in. wide, c.1780. £450-550 PH

An Irish pine corner cupboard, with sunburst interior. £500-600 RC

A pine corner cupboard, restored with old wood, 72in. high, 27in. wide, 12in. deep. £125-150 WH

An 18th C. pine corner cupboard, 75in. high, 24in. wide. £225-250 GLF

A late Georgian pine full length standing corner cupboard, 39in. wide. £350-400

A pine corner cupboard, with barrel back and shaped shelves, 79in. high, c.1840. £575-650 Ad

An astragal glazed, barrel backed pine corner cupboard, 80in. high, c.1840. £400-500 AL

A pine bow-fronted double corner cupboard, 9ft. 6in. high, c.1850. £300-350 PH

A Georgian pine corner cupboard, with two panelled doors and shaped shelves, 73in. high, 36in. wide. £300-350 AH

A Victorian pine double corner cupboard, 34in. wide, 82in. high. £250-300 Co

A pine double corner cupboard, 6ft. 3in. high, 3ft. 1in. wide, c.1850. £475-500 PH

A 19th C. Welsh pine and fruitwood glazed corner cupboard, with two shaped shelves, 3ft. 6in. wide, 6ft. high. £400-500

A mid 19th C. free-standing full length pine corner cupboard, 6ft. 4in. high, 3ft. wide. £400-450 MV

A Georgian pine hanging corner cupboard, with one door and shaped shelves, 35in. wide, 46in. high. £130-160 AH

A 19th C. Welsh pine narrow corner cupboard, with glazed top and cupboard below, 6ft. 4in. high, 2ft. 6in. wide. £350-400

A late 18th C. pine corner cupboard, 36in. wide. £150-200   Bed

A pine corner cupboard, 31½in. high, 27in. wide, 17½in. deep, c.1840. £155-175   W

A 19th C. pine corner cupboard, with applied moulding to door, 31in. wide, 44in. high. £140-170

A Georgian pine hanging corner cupboard, 24in. high. £125-150   Co

A small 17th C. pine wall cupboard, with original hinges, 23in. high, 25in. wide. £120-160

A 19th C. fruitwood corner cupboard, with panelled doors, 31in. wide, 44in. high. £140-170

A 19th C. pine and elm corner cupboard, with inscribed carving on each door 'God is faithful' and 'Love one another', 27in. high, 20in. wide. £100-150

A pine hanging wall cupboard, 12½in. wide, 18in. high, 5½in. deep, c.1850. £30-40   AL

A pine hanging glazed cupboard, 30in. wide, 36in. high, 9in. deep. £45-55   DPN

A pine display cabinet, 39in. high, 27½in. wide, 7½in. deep, c.1780. £190-220

A Welsh pine bedside cupboard, 31in. high, 17in. wide, 15in. deep, c.1860. £60-70 Sca

A 19th C. pitch pine glazed cupboard, 48in. high, 41in. wide, 14in. deep. £75-100 GLF

A Victorian pine pot cupboard, 18in. square. £50-60 AL

A mid Victorian pine pot cupboard, with single drawer, 18in. square. £75-95 AL

A pine glazed hanging cabinet, 15 by 8 by 18in. £75-100 Bed

A Victorian pine bedside cupboard, 16in. wide. £50-70

A Regency pine tambour-fronted bedside cupboard, 18in. wide, c.1820. £80-100 AL

A 19th C. pine wall cupboard, with four drawers above cupboard and applied decoration, 26in. wide, 29in. high, 7in. deep. £80-100

A 19th C. pine hanging cupboard, with galleried upper shelf and original handle, 27in. wide, 19in. high, 6in. deep. £40-60

A pine pot cupboard, 15½in. wide, c.1850. £60-80 W

107

A Victorian pine bedside cupboard, 16in. wide. £50-65

A pine pot cupboard, with original porcelain handle, 14in. wide, 30in. high, 13½in. deep. £50-60 AL

A late Victorian pine bedside table, 16in. wide. £60-80.

A Scandinavian pine pot cupboard, 19½in. wide, c.1890. £55-65 W

A pine bedside cupboard, with lifting top, 2ft. 6in. high, 1ft. 6in. wide, c.1890. £60-70 BEL

A Scandinavian pine pot cupboard, 18in. wide, c.1890. £55-75

A pine bedside cabinet, 15in. square, 2ft. 6in. high, c.1860. £55-65 AL

A late Victorian pine pot cupboard, 32in. high, 15in. wide, 12½in. deep. £75-85 W

A Scandinavian pine pot cupboard, with original fittings, lift up top, 20in. wide, c.1890. £60-80 W

An Edwardian pine bedside cupboard on turned legs, 34in. high, 24in. deep, 24in. wide. £60-70

A 19th C. pine bread proving cupboard, on original castors, 41in. wide, 48in. high. £120-140

A pine proving cupboard, back missing, 3ft. 10in. wide, c.1840. £110-130   AL

A pine proving cupboard, tin lined, 3ft. 4in. wide, 3ft. 8in. high, c.1840. £100-130   AL

A late 19th C. pine corner cupboard, 48in. high, 32in. wide, £195-240   Ad

An 18th C. miniature pine cupboard, with a fielded panel door, 16in. wide, 17½in. high, 10in. deep. £95-115

A small 20th C. amateur made pine cabinet, 18in. high, 10in. wide. £20-25

A 19th . pine pot cupboard, 31in. high, 16in. wide. £50-60   Ad

An astragal glazed pine corner cabinet, 22in. wide, 33in. high, c.1825. £140-160   Bed

A Georgian pine open top corner cupboard, with fluted sides and shaped shelves, 82in. high, 44in. wide. £300-320

A Georgian pine hanging corner cupboard, 31in. high. £100-125   Co

Desks

The writing desk has its origin in the scriptoria of mediaeval monasteries. As few people could write in those days, not much thought was given to the design and production of the desk.

Over the centuries, as literacy increased, so did the variety and elegance of desks; the peak being reached during the Regency and Victorian periods. During the Victorian period, many pine desks were produced, ranging from large partners' desks to the smaller kneehole variety. As with most pine furniture, good quality, small pieces in original condition sell well.

There is a large demand from both the European and American market for good small pine desks and hence these can be expensive.

Many desks were destroyed in the early years of this century as the telephone and car put paid to the art of letter writing. This scarcity coupled with the obvious demand has led to many desks being produced from old pine. Some of these are well-made and, as long as the price is right, should not be disregarded.

An 18th C. pine desk on stand, with applied mouldings on desk front and fitted interior, 3ft. high, 2ft. 4in. wide. £275-300   DH

A 19th C. pitch pine desk, with side flap and two porcelain inkwells, 36in. high, 33in. wide, 24in. deep. £110-130   AL

A pine bureau, 3ft. 7in. by 1ft. 8in. by 3ft. 7in. high, c.1840. £525-550   PCA

A pine desk, 29in. wide, 44in. high, c.1850. £100-120   AL

A 19th C. Scandinavian pine cylinder top bureau, awaiting handles and final polishing, with interior drawers and writing slope, 4ft. 2in. wide, 3ft. 10in. high, 23in. deep, price as finished. £600-700

A Georgian pine estate desk on stand, the interior with three drawers, 24in. wide. £170-230

A Victorian pine davenport, 24½in. wide, 41in. high, c.1850. £280-340   AL

A pine bureau, 42in. high, 41in. wide, 17½in. deep, c.1830. £675-725

A Danish pine bureau chest escritoire, 50in. high, 41in. wide, 19in. deep, c.1840. £600-650   WH

A small Georgian pine bureau, 3ft. high, 33in. wide. £600-700   PH

A 19th C. pitch pine clerk's desk, 40in. high, 21in. deep, 24in. wide. £90-110

A pine breakfront kneehole desk, 47in. wide, 33in. high, 23in. deep, c.1860. £350-400   AL

A small Georgian pine kneehole desk, with nine drawers, central cupboard, 4ft. wide, 19in. deep. £400-425   MV

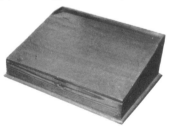

A 19th C. pine writing slope, with hinged lid, interior not fitted, 19in. wide, 15in. deep. £30-35

A 19th C. pine pedestal desk, with nine drawers, 22in. deep, 46in wide. £300-400

A pine flat top desk, 19in. wide, 24in. deep, 12in. high, c.1850. £20-30   AL

A 19th C. pine desk top, with fitted interior, 33in. wide, 24in. deep. £60-70

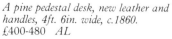

A pine pedestal desk, new leather and handles, 4ft. 6in. wide, c.1860. £400-480   AL

A 19th C. corn merchant's desk, in pearwood, with six drawers, and central inset cupboard, 45in. wide, 21in. deep, 44in. high. £350-400

A pine desk, 36in. wide, 44in. high, 17½in. deep, c.1840. £270-300 AL

A Victorian pine pedestal desk, 48in. wide. £320-360 AL

A Victorian pine desk, hinged top, the doors hiding two sets of sliding trays, 4ft. wide. £180-220 AL

A pine davenport, with drawers in the side, 3ft. high, 2ft. wide, c.1850. £350-400 RK

A pine kneehole desk, 32in. high, 4ft 4in. wide, 18in. deep, c.1850. £250-275 PH

A Victorian pine kneehole desk, with eight drawers and central inset cupboard, on bracket feet, 31in. high, 34in. wide, 19in. deep. £345-395 AH

A 19th C. pine desk, with fretwork sides, three drawers and pigeonholes, 39in. wide, 21in. deep. £250-300

A pine school desk, 24 by 21in. £75-100 Bed

A 19th C. pine bow-fronted desk, with nine drawers and gesso decoration, 53in. wide, 27in. deep. £650-700

A small 19th C. Scandinavian pine writing desk, with drawer and lifting top, 2ft. 7in. high, 2ft. 5in. wide. £125-150 BEL

A 19th C. pine secretaire, 58½in. high, 40in. wide, 17in. deep. £450-475 W

A pine desk, 2ft. 5in. high, 3ft. 1in. wide. £125-150 BEL

A Victorian pine pedestal desk, 38in. wide. £300-325 Co

A 19th C. pine escritoire, with ten interior drawers and new Chippendale-style handles and escutcheons, 56in. high, 39in. wide. £400-450

A Victorian pine desk, new leather top, 49in. wide. £250-300 Far

A pine escritoire, 37in. wide, c.1890. £395-450 W

An English pine desk, 34in. high, 48in. wide, 28in. deep, c.1840. £300-350 PH

An Edwardian pitch pine pedestal desk, three drawers with swan neck handles and two cupboards with fielded panelled doors, 46in. wide, 19in. deep. £300-350

A pine pedestal desk, 2ft. 7in. high, 4ft. 1in. wide, 2ft. deep. £160-180 BEL

A pine pedestal desk, 30 by 48 by 23in. £340-360 Bed

113

A 19th C. 'Faux Bamboo' pine kneehole desk, 51in. wide. £375-425   D

A 19th C. pine kneehole desk, with three drawers and two cupboards, 42in. wide, 23in. deep. £290-330   D

A Victorian pine bow-fronted desk, with one drawer, two cupboards and gesso decoration, 30in. high, 52in. wide, 23in. deep. £290-340   AH

An example of a 19th C. pine chest of drawers, converted into a bureau, 3ft. 8in. high, 3ft. wide. £175-200   RK

A Scandinavian pine bureau, 110cm. high, 107cm. wide. £450-550   BEL

An Edwardian pine clerks' desk, with four drawers and single cupboard, 50in. high, 43in. wide, 18in. deep. £250-275   PJ

A pine roll-top desk, 36 by 20in. £175-200   Bed

A Scandinavian pine secretaire, 112cm. high, 98cm. wide. £350-450   BEL

Mirrors

In the early seventeenth century, man's vanity decreed that the polished metal mirror was not of sufficient quality and clarity. Hence the first silvered-glass mirrors were introduced into Britain in 1615. The quality of the reflection was, by today's standards, extremely poor.

However there is a certain charm to old mirror glass and, if in reasonable condition, this should always be preserved as it can add considerably to the value of the piece.

The Victorians produced a large number of mirrors which were generally of extremely high quality. These have increased in price quite considerably over the last few years as they were certainly under-valued – to the extent of being cheaper than their modern equivalents.

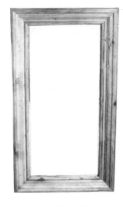

A Victorian pine mirror frame, 38in. high. £35-45   Far

A 19th C. pine framed mirror, 30 by 30 in. £70-90

A pine framed mirror, 34in. wide, c.1830. £90-125   Far

A Victorian pine dressing table mirror, with carved mirror supports and carved feet, 24in. high, 19in. wide. £60-80

A Victorian pine framed mirror, 28 by 24in. £40-50   AH

A Victorian pine framed mirror, 18in. wide. £20-30   Far

A 19th C. wall mirror, with bevelled glass and gesso decoration on pine surround, 45in. high, 32in. wide. £100-120

A pine overmantel mirror, with gesso decoration, 26in. high, 60in. wide. £60-80 PJ

A 19th C. pine overmantel mirror, with scratch carving, 34in. high, 48in. wide. £40-50 AL

A Victorian pine dressing mirror, with oval box in base, 19in. high, 15in. wide. £70-90

A small dressing mirror, with drawer, 19in. high, 15in. wide, 8in. deep. £70-90

A pine framed wall-hanging mirror, 60in. high. c.1890. £75-100 W

A beech framed toilet mirror, 28½in. high. £45-75 W

A 19th C. pine overmantel mirror, with gesso decoration, 36in. high, 50 in. wide. £85-105

A pair of 19th C. pine mirrors, and shelves, 12in. £30-40 AL

A pine carved overmantel, with mirror in central arch and double, turned support pillars, 5ft. high, 4ft. 4in. wide, 12in. deep, c.1888. £300-350

A 19th C. French pine folding three-panel mirror. £65-95

A Victorian pine overmantel mirror, 40in. wide. £30-40 Far

A 19th C. pine picture mirror frame, 30 by 30in. £70-90

A 19th C. pine overmantel mirror, 36in. high, 33in. wide. £60-90

Shelves

Small sets of hanging shelves have been in use since the sixteenth century. As with most furniture of this period, these were normally of very basic design with no pretentions to elegance. They were functional and little thought was given to their external appearance.

During the seventeenth century, they tended to spread in width and became much more decorative. Thomas Chippendale not only designed shelves specifically for books but also made these small pieces of furniture decorative masterpieces.

As with most sections in this book, pine was used for the more utilitarian pieces. This does not detract at all from the value of small cupboards and shelves in pine as they are still useful and often attractive additions to the modern décor.

A set of late 19th C. pine wall hanging corner shelves, with shaped sides and front, 30in. high. £60-80

A set of 18th C. pine hanging bookshelves, with shaped sides and narrow reeded cornice, 31in. high, 35in. wide, 7in. deep. £80-110

A pine shelf unit, 31in. high, 20in. wide, 12in. deep. £30-40   AL

A set of pine shelves, 5ft. 2in. high, 4ft. 6in. wide, c.1870. £70-80   AL

A pine hanging wall shelf, with brass end finials, 16in. high, 21in. wide, 6½in. deep, c.1860. £40-50   AL

A set of pine shelves, 3ft. high, 2ft. 6in. wide, c.1870. £60-70   AL

A pine reproduction standing or hanging rack, made to order, any size or design, in old wood. Price range £35 up. As shown £80 SW

A set of 19th C. pine hanging bookshelves, with shaped sides and divided lower shelf, 39in. high, 26in. wide, 8in. deep. £55-75

A pine hanging wall shelf, 21½in. high, 27½in. wide, 4½in. deep, c.1860. £40-50 AL

A set of pine shelves, 42in. high, 31in. wide, 8in. deep, c.1860. £55-65 AL

A set of 19th C. pine hanging shelves, with shaped sides, of deep golden colour, 16in. high, 18in. wide, 5in. deep. £45-55

An Irish pine wall rack, 46in. high, 37in. wide, 12½in. deep, c.1800. £150-175 HH

A 20th C. small pine bookcase, with contrasting turnings on each set of bars, 38in. high, 18in. wide. £70-90

A set of pine bookshelves, 28in. high, 21in. wide, 6in. deep. £50-60 HH

A pine wall rack, with carved and shaped corbels, applied bow and bell carving to centre, 42in. high, 36in. wide. £75-100   GHM

A set of pine bookshelves, 48in. high, 27in. wide, 6in. deep, c.1860. £50-60   AL

A late Georgian pine bookcase, 37in. wide. £200-250

A pine delft rack, 3ft. high, 3ft. 4in. wide, 8in. deep. £90-100   CRP

An early Victorian pine delft rack, 43in. wide. £110-160

A pine corner unit, 35in. high, 31in. wide, 18½in. deep, c.1860. £50-60   AL

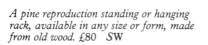

A pine reproduction standing or hanging rack, available in any size or form, made from old wood. £80   SW

A tall pine shelf unit, 45in. high, 41in. wide, 18in. deep, c.1860. £40-50   AL

A set of Victorian pine hanging shelves, with shaped sides, 29in. high, 25in. wide, 8in. deep. £40-55   AH

Settles

In mediaeval times almost the only forms of seating were crude stools, benches and chests. The interior of a mediaeval home was extremely sparse, with little of comfort available. Chests and benches were usually placed against walls and benches were not uncommonly fixed to the panelling of lordly establishments.

Once this is realised, the ancestry of the settle is immediately apparent, for it is no more than a bench or chest fitted with its own small section of wall panelling and equipped with arms.

These useful pieces of furniture often had a cupboard under the seat. The bacon settle or bacon cupboard is a variation on the same theme, combining a wide, shallow cupboard with the settle back. This, as the name suggests, was used for food storage.

In the nineteenth century, a large number of provincial settles were made in pine and smaller examples are at a premium.

A pine settle, with cupboards below the seat, 45in. high, 55in. wide, 20in. deep. £175-200 DPN

A pine settle, with panelled back, 144cm. high, 194cm. wide, 52cm. deep, c.1790. £400-500 SAL

An 18th C. pine settle, with fielded panels, 4ft. high, 52in. wide. £300-350

A 19th C. Welsh pine box settle, 64in. wide. £280-320 Co

An 18th C. pine bacon settle, with original iron hooks inside, probably Welsh, 5ft. 9in. high, 4ft. 6in. wide. £1,600-1,700 Jos

An 18th C. pine settle, with wide planked back, 50in. high. £200-250

A Welsh small pine settle, with a box in the base, 4ft. high, 4ft. wide, 20in. deep, c.1850. £300-350

A pine settle, 67in. high, 14in. deep, c.1840. £900-1,000 W

A Welsh pine monks settle, 4ft. 6in. wide, c.1820. £400-500 RK
The top folds forward over the arms to make a table.

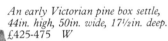

A pine peg-joined box settle, 4ft. high, 4ft. wide, c.1750. £300-350

An early Victorian pine box settle, 44in. high, 50in. wide, 17½in. deep. £425-475 W

A Somerset pine settle, with cupboards in the back, 5ft. 10in. high, 5ft. 6in. wide, 21in. deep, c.1840. £650-750

A late 19th C. Welsh pitch pine box settle, 56in. high, 54in. wide, 20in. deep. £380-420 MV

Steps

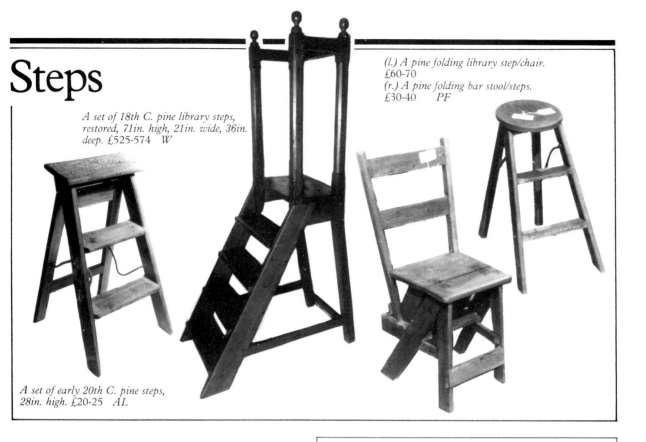

A set of 18th C. pine library steps, restored, 71in. high, 21in. wide, 36in. deep. £525-574 W

(l.) A pine folding library step/chair. £60-70
(r.) A pine folding bar stool/steps. £30-40 PF

A set of early 20th C. pine steps, 28in. high. £20-25 AL

A pine barrel backed settle, 6ft. wide, c.1840. £325-375 AL

A pine convent seat, 87 by 147 by 30cm. £80-95 SAL

Stools

*A 19th C. beech and elm stool, 18in. high.
£20-25   AL*

*A late 19th C. kitchen stool in beech,
with turned legs and crossed stretchers,
21in. high. £25-30*

*A late 19th C. beech kitchen stool,
21in. high. £20-25*

*A 19th C. small stool, with turned pine
legs and oak top, 10in. wide, 7in. deep.
£12-15*

*An 18th C. pine joint stool, with restored
top. £45-55*

*A 19th C. Welsh pine spinning stool,
24in. high. £40-45   PF*

A pine stool, 20in. high. £20-25   AL

*A late Georgian elm and ash stool,
18in. wide. £20-25*

*An early 19th C. pitch pine footstool,
12 by 6in. £10-15*

*A pine stool, on turned legs, 28in. high.
£25-30   AL*

*An 18th C. elm country made stool.
£30-40   D*

An 18th C. fruitwood milking stool.
£55-65

An early 18th C. pine joint stool, with
pegged top. £350-400 Jos

A late Victorian pine stool, 27in. high,
12in. wide. £55-60 W

A 19th C. elm stool, 12in. high.
£18-20 AL

A 19th C. pitch pine footstool, 12in. wide,
6in. deep. £10-15

A Victorian sycamore stool, 12in. high.
£25-30 W

A pine stool, 24in. high. £20-25 AL

A 19th C. pine school bench, 8ft. long.
£45-50

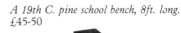

A pair of 19th C. pitch pine stools,
18½in. £60-65 AL

A 19th C. pine stool, 12in. high.
£18-20 AL

A 19th C. pine stool. £18-22 AH

A beech pew, 72in. long. £70-80 DPN

A 19th C. small elm stool, on close-turned
legs. £30-35

A 19th C. pine bench table, 84in. long,
23in. deep. £130-150

Tables

Of all pieces of furniture produced throughout the centuries, few can have been made to serve such a diversity of specific purposes as the table. Size, shape, style, construction: all have been manipulated and permutated in the interests of function and fashion.

Tables vary from the workmanlike solidity of a thick-topped bench table to the 'cottagey' simplicity of the pine cricket table, and from the expansive dependability of the spindle legged tea tables that proliferated from the mid eighteenth century.

Pine has always been a popular wood for tables, particularly the more rustic examples. Pine side tables in particular have been found to fit ideally into the modern home and where would the 'cottagey' pine kitchen be without the compulsory pine table?

A word about reproduction pine tables: – there is a strong demand for circular period pine kitchen tables but these were not produced in large quantities. Many high quality new or made-up tables are produced but it is worth going to a reputable dealer who will guarantee his work.

An early pine pegged straight leg table, 37½ by 26in. top, c.1830. £50-60   AL

An early 19th C. pine kitchen table, the two drawers with cup handles, 60in. long, 30in. wide. £100-150

A Victorian pine kitchen table, on turned legs, 36in long, 24in. wide. £75-95   AH

An Irish pine dairy table, 31in. high, 11ft. long, 39in. wide, c.1820. £450-500   HH

A long Irish pine stretcher table, 8ft. 6in. by 3ft., c.1850 £350-400   PH

A late Georgian Irish pine stretcher table, 30in. high, 96in. long, 36in. wide. £400-450   PF

An Irish pine stretcher table, 30in. high, 4ft. 6in. long, 2ft. 2in. wide. £130-170 SW
The style suggests early 19th C. but probably later, say 1880.

An Irish pine country table, with double rail, 4ft. 8in. long, 25in. wide, c.1850. £120-150

A 19th C. long narrow pine table, of deep golden colour, with turned legs, 31in. high, 87in. long, 24in. wide. £350-400

An Irish pine country table, with cross stretcher, 4ft. long, 28in. wide, c.1860. £85-100 RK

A Victorian pine wind-out table, on turned legs, 38 by 38in. closed, 38 by 60in. opened. £160-190 AH

A Victorian pine three-plank farmhouse kitchen table, 8ft., c.1870. £225-275

A small pine table, with one drawer, 29in. high, 35in. long, 23in. wide. £50-60 AL

A Victorian pitch pine table, with one drawer and turned legs, 48in. long, 30in. wide. £140-170 AH

A pine farmhouse kitchen table, 7ft. long, c.1870. £225-275

A 19th C. plain pine kitchen table, on turned legs, 43in. long, 30in. wide. £55-60

A 19th C. large pine table on castors, 30in. high, 60in. long, 42in. wide. £160-180

An 18th C. pine Sutherland table, 20cm. unextended, 106cm. extended, 86cm. wide. £150-250 SAL

A 19th C. elm table, 29in. high, 36in. long, 18in. wide. £40-50 GLF

An unusual 19th C. Scandinavian pine oval table, 30in. high, 51in. long, 34in. wide. £425-475 W

A Victorian pine extending dining table, with single leaf, 3ft. 3in. by 5ft. fully extended. £250-300

A late Victorian pine table, 35in. deep. £60-65 Far

A 19th C. pine refectory table, with sturdy centre stretchers and supports and shaped top rails, 60in. long, 33in. wide. £180-220

A Victorian pine table, 39in. diam. £50-65 AL

A round table, with fruitwood top, pine skirt and oak legs, 30in. high, 56in. diam., c.1790. £350-450 HH
This table folds in half to become D-shaped.

An early Victorian pine kitchen table, 29in. high, 4ft. long, 21in. wide, c.1840. £95-120 SW
Note the deep turning and cut up sides.

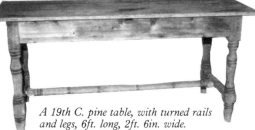

A 19th C. pine table, with turned rails and legs, 6ft. long, 2ft. 6in. wide. £270-300

A 19th C. pine table, 29in. high, 54in. long, 36in. wide. £90-100 GLF

A pine drop-leaf table, with drawer, 29in. high, 19in. long closed, 34in. open, 35in. wide, c.1860. £65-75 AL

A pine D-end table, consisting of five tables which clip together, originally simulated mahogany, 10ft. long, 3ft. 6in. wide. £1,400-1,500 Jos

A French pine wine table, with an oval top, 5ft. 10in. long, 3ft. 7in. wide, c.1850. £300-400 PH

A Victorian pine one-flap table, with two frieze drawers, 4ft. by 3ft. open. £140-190

A 19th C. pine kitchen table, with one gate-leg and two drawers, 29in. high, 34in. long, open, 18in. closed, 42in. wide. £90-110

A pine single flap table, with drawer, original porcelain handles, 28in. high, 36in. long, 22in. wide, c.1850. £60-70 AL

A small pine drop-leaf table, 29in. high, 19in. wide closed, 29in. wide open, 26in. long, c.1840. £60-70 AL

A Victorian Cotswold pine single drop-leaf table, with extending frame, 36 by 37in. extended. £100-150

A pine two drawer single leaf table, 30in. high, 55in. long, 28½in. deep, 37½in. deep with leaf. £125-135 AL

A pine gateleg table, 33 by 47½in., c.1840. £120-150 AL

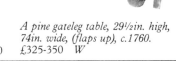

A 19th C. pine gateleg table, 30in. high, 52in. long, open, 34in. wide. £145-165 GLF

A 19th C. pine drop-leaf table, with one drawer and on turned legs, 18in. long closed, 33in. extended, 39in. wide. £80-100

A pine gateleg table, 29½in. high, 74in. wide, (flaps up), c.1760. £325-350 W

An Irish pine circular table, 36in. high, 34in. diam., c.1820. £60-80   WH

A Victorian pine table, 48in. long, opening to 43in. wide, c.1880. £80-100   Far

A pine table, 30in. high, 36in. long, 21½in. wide, c.1720. £300-350   W

A pine circular drop-leaf table, on slim turned legs, 40in. diam., c.1850-1890. £180-200

A small Scandinavian pine drop-leaf table, 37in. diam., c.1900. £60-75   W

A Regency pine side table, with 'bamboo' legs, original handles, 3ft. wide, c.1820. £70-85   AL

A pine drop-leaf table, 45in. extended, c.1880. £65-85   Far

A chunky Victorian pine drop-leaf table, with one end drawer and turned legs, 30in. wide, 17in. closed, 34in. extended. £60-70

A Georgian pine side table, 29in. high, 42in. long, 19in. wide. £140-160   PF

A 19th C. pine table, 35in. diam. £70-100   WH

A Swedish pine gateleg table, 2ft. 8in. high, 6ft. 6in. long, 3ft. 5in. wide, c.1850. £200-230   PCA

A 19th C. pine small table, 29in. high, 22in. wide. £30-50   GLF

A pine side table, 2ft. 11in. wide, c.1840. £60-70   AL

A pine side table, on tapered legs, 29in. high, 33in. long, 19in. wide, c.1850. £75-95   HH

A pine table, with two drawers, original handles, 29in. high, 40in. long, 24in. wide, c.1840. £90-100   AL

An early 19th C. pine country made side table, with one drawer and sturdy, tapered legs, 29in. high, 38in. long, 19in. wide. £50-70

A pine side table, 35½in. wide, c.1890. £50-70   Far

A pine side table, 35in. wide, c.1840. £60-70

A Georgian pine side table, with one drawer and squared tapered legs, 31in. high, 35in. long, 17in. wide. £110-135   AH

A Victorian pine side table, with simulated bamboo legs, 30in. wide. £80-100

A pine two drawer side table, with new handles, 30in. high, 41in. long, 21in. wide. £85-95   AL

A pine side table, 39in. £100-150   WH

A Georgian pine side table, 32in. wide. £120-150

An Irish pine side table, 4ft. by 2ft. 2in., c.1860. £130-140   PCA

A 19th C. pine side table, with one drawer and on bobbin turned legs, 41in. long, 18in. wide. £80-100

A small 19th C. pine side table, with one drawer and turned legs, 28in. long, 17in. wide. £40-50

A 19th C. Devonshire pine table, with tapered legs and shaped top rail, 30 in. high, 9ft. long, 3ft. 3in. wide. £400-450

A mid 19th C pine console table, with heavily carved front legs and shield decoration to back, 40in. high, 3ft. 9in. long, 20in. wide. £200-250

A pine side table, 28in. high, 35½in. long, 18½in. wide, c.1860 £55-65   AL

A 19th C. pine side table, with one drawer and porcelain handles, 36in. long, 24in. wide. £45-50   AL

A pine lyre-end writing table, 29in. high, 39in. long, 19in. wide. £130-160   PF

A pine side table, with original porcelain handles, 29in. high, 33in. long, 17in. wide, c.1850. £50-60   AL

A Welsh pine drop-leaf table, with one drawer and ogee scroll each end, 30in. wide, 33in. extended. £95-125   PF

A Victorian pine writing table, 39in. wide. £150-180

A Victorian pine table, 30in. wide, c.1880. £60-70   Far

A pair of pine tables, with delicately turned legs, 29in. high, 42in. long, 22in. wide. £50-60 each   AL

A small pine side table, c.1850.
£50-60   Ad

A pine table, with turned legs, 28in. high,
33in. long, 16in. wide, c.1860.
£45-55   AL

An Edwardian pine side table, with
replacement handles, 29in. high, 3ft. long,
2ft. wide, c.1900.
£85-100   SW
Note the cut turnings in the bowls –
this is an easy dating guide.

A Victorian pine side table, 42in. wide,
c.1860. £60-70   Far

A pine side table, 32 by 15in.
£90-100   Bed

An Edwardian pine writing table, with
three drawers, 30in. high, 48in. long,
30 in wide. £275-300   W

A pine folding top tea trolley, 28in. high,
24in. long, 17in. wide. £70-80   PF

A mid Victorian pine side table, with
original handles, 42in. wide. £70-100   W

A pine side table, 29 by 18 by 29in.
£80-100   Bed

A mid Victorian pine side table, 36in.
wide. £60-70

An Edwardian pine side table, 36in. wide.
£70-80   Co

A pair of pine corner console tables, with
marble tops, 30in. high. £950-1,000   Jos

A small Spanish pine table, with shaped side rails and one deep drawer, 24in. high, 24in. long, 18in. wide. £130-170

A 19th C. fruitwood occasional table, originally one of a nest of three, 27in. high, 16in. long, 12in. wide. £90-110

A pine tripod table, with brass banded top cut across tree, and a Georgian base. £350-400 Jos

A 20th C. small pine occasional table, with fretwork side rails and scallop edged table top, 25in. high, 22in. wide, 15in. deep. £40-50

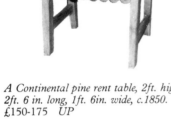

A Continental pine rent table, 2ft. high, 2ft. 6 in. long, 1ft. 6in. wide, c.1850. £150-175 UP

A Victorian pine cricket table, 20in. diam. £60-80

A pine side table, 26in. high, 25in. long, 18in. wide. £90-100 Sca

A Victorian pine table, 30in. high, 19in. wide. £140-160 W

A 19th C. stripped pine sewing table, the exterior originally lacquered, with original lacquered fitted interior, 24in. wide, 16in. deep. £250-300

A pine bench table, 24in. high, 26in. long, 13in. wide, c.1860. £40-50 AL

A pine octagonal wine table, 17½in. wide, c.1900. £65-95 W

A Victorian pine bakers' work table, with two deep drawers and shelf under, 32in. high, 38in. wide, 20in. deep. £130-160   AH

A pine console table, 82cm. high, 66cm. wide, 31cm. deep. £220-250   SAL

A 19th C. pine trestle table, with iron stretcher, 54in. long, 18in. wide. £120-150

A 19th C. Welsh cricket table, in pine and ash, 29in. diam. £100-120

A Victorian pine cricket table, 20in. diam. £75-115

A late 18th C. pine cricket table, 26in. diam. £85-105

A pine cricket table, 2ft. 6in. diam., c.1810. £100-120   AL

A Tyrolean pine centre table, with hinged moulded rectangular plank top, with later interior above the carved frieze on solid panelled and carved trestle supports, joined by stretchers and stepped feet, 41in. (104cm.) wide, basically 18th C. £2,000-2,500   C

A pine small round country table, 2ft. high, 1ft. 4in. diam of top. £30-40   CRP

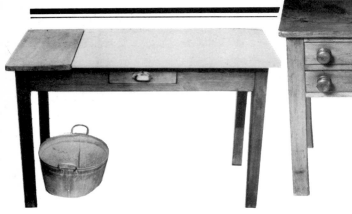

A mid 19th C. fish filleting table, marble topped with lifting wooden flap, 3ft. 6in. long. £140-160   AL

A pine press table, 20in. wide, c.1860. £50-60   AL

An unusual 19th C. pine small folding card table, with engraved decoration, probably Russian. £280-320   RK

A pine bakers' table, with marble top, 36 by 30 by 37in. £140-160   Bed

A 19th C. bakers' trolley on large wooden castors, 3ft. square. £90-120   AL

A Victorian pine 'tip top' breakfast table, on carved mahogany feet, 33in. diam. £135-155   D

A 19th C. pine Pembroke table, with cutlery drawer at one end, on turned legs, 29in. high, 18 by 36in. top, extending to 30 by 36in. £50-70   PCo

A large early 19th C. pine table, with side drawers, 78in. long. £350-395   D

Miscellaneous

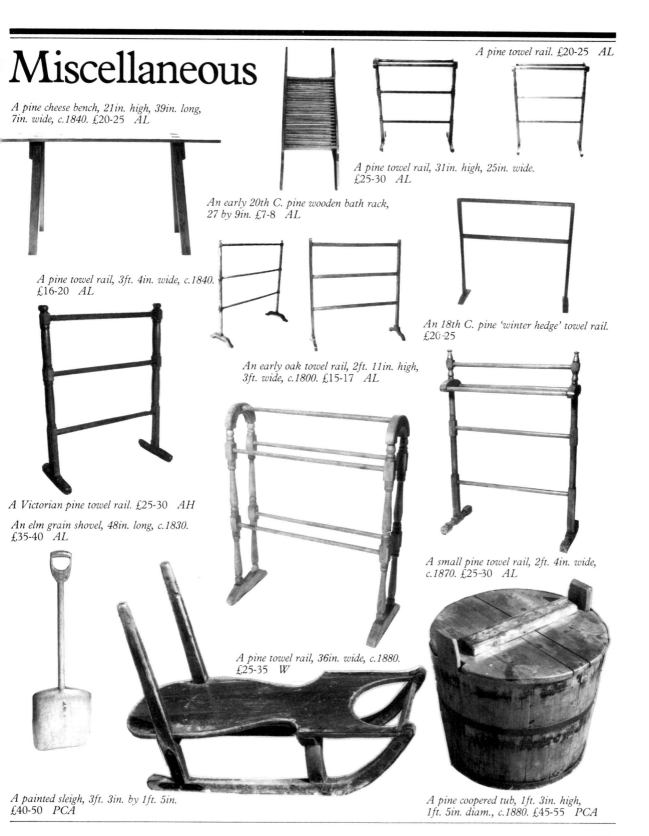

A pine cheese bench, 21in. high, 39in. long, 7in. wide, c.1840. £20-25   AL

A pine towel rail. £20-25   AL

A pine towel rail, 31in. high, 25in. wide. £25-30   AL

An early 20th C. pine wooden bath rack, 27 by 9in. £7-8   AL

A pine towel rail, 3ft. 4in. wide, c.1840. £16-20   AL

An 18th C. pine 'winter hedge' towel rail. £20-25

An early oak towel rail, 2ft. 11in. high, 3ft. wide, c.1800. £15-17   AL

A Victorian pine towel rail. £25-30   AH

An elm grain shovel, 48in. long, c.1830. £35-40   AL

A small pine towel rail, 2ft. 4in. wide, c.1870. £25-30   AL

A pine towel rail, 36in. wide, c.1880. £25-35   W

A painted sleigh, 3ft. 3in. by 1ft. 5in. £40-50   PCA

A pine coopered tub, 1ft. 3in. high, 1ft. 5in. diam., c.1880. £45-55   PCA

A pine towel rail, c.1900. £18-25

A Continental pine pestle and mortar, spoon and spice rack, with pestle and mortar, 2ft. 2in. wide, c.1870. £70-85 PCA

An Edwardian beech towel rail, 25in. £15-20

A Continental pine grain shoot, 2ft. 6in. £30-40 PCA

A Victorian pine work box, 21in. wide. £120-150

An early Continental pine hook board, 6ft. 3in. long, 9½in. wide. £80-100 PCA

An East German pine fruit press, 21in. high, 24in. across top, 7¾in. wide, c.1800. £50-100 WH

A small pine plant stand, 3ft. high, 1ft. 2in. wide, 1ft. deep, c.1840. £25-35 AL

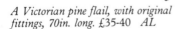

A Victorian pine flail, with original fittings, 70in. long. £35-40 AL

A Continental pine bottle rack and bottles, 3ft. 6in. c.1850. £130-140 PCA

An Irish pine spit rack, 4ft. 6in. high, 4ft. wide. £130-150 GF

A 19th C. pine vegetable rack, with four compartments of varying depths, sturdy construction, 36in. high, 15in. wide. £45-55

A 19th C. Welsh pine ham rack, with decorative chamfered edges. £85-100 COR

A pine fire surround, 43 by 46in. £125-150 Bed

A pine refrigerator, with zinc lining, made by Belmont, box for ice at top, 38in. high, 18in. wide, c.1870. £100-120

A pine butchers' block, 36in. high, 60in. long, 24in. wide. £300-350 PF

A Victorian pine fire surround, with heavy turned and moulded side supports, 4ft. 2in. high, 6ft. wide. £150-170

A pine Adam style fire surround, 51in. high, 56in. wide. £450-550 Sca

A 19th C. pine mantelpiece, 130cm. high, 166cm. wide. £115-130 SAL

A pine plant stand, 3ft. high, 3ft. 6in. wide, 1ft. deep. £70-80 CRP

An Edwardian pine over-mantel, with dentil moulding and bevelled mirrors, 60in. wide. £125-150 D

A pine planter, 31in. high, 32in. wide, 19in. deep, c.1860. £375-400 W

A pine fire surround, 4ft. high by 4ft. 1in. by 8in. £160-190 PCA

A pine fireplace, with applied carved swags and acanthus centre piece in lime fluted sides, heavily moulded top, 4ft. high, 44in. wide. £175-200 GHM

A pine wheel mould, 26in. diam., c.1850. £40-50 PH

A late 19th C. pine shop counter, with inset panel front, 32in. high, 60in. long. £80-100

An elm and pine wheelbarrow, 46in. long, c.1850. £60-80 AL

An elm wheelbarrow, with a wrought iron wheel, 5ft. long, c.1860. £90-110 AL

A pine free-standing counter, 2ft. 10½in. high, 3ft. 8in. long, 1ft. 7in. wide. £75-100 CRP

A 19th C. pine dog, one of a pair, male and female, 40in. high. £650-700 Jos

A 19th C. pine shop counter, with two deep drawers, 36in. high, 54in. long, 32in. wide. £150-200

A brass gong on pine stand, 4ft. high, c.1860. £75-85 AL

A Victorian pine screen, 70in. high. £40-45 AL

A Scandinavian pine spinning wheel, in working condition, 37in. high, c.1840. £125-175 W

A pair of Italian stripped pine wall brackets. £200-250

An 18th C. pine wall bracket, in the shape of a lion. £110-135 SAL

A Scandinavian pine spinning wheel, 3ft. high, c.1860. £165-190 PCA

A pair of pine Adam style wall brackets, 12in. diam. £750-800 Jos

A pine flax loom, 58in. high, 24in. wide, c.1800. £75-85 WH

A late 19th C. pine spinning wheel and spindle. £160-190 W

A Victorian schoolroom abacus, on pine base and frame with slate on reverse side. £48-55 COR

A late 19th C. pine pulpit, 3ft. 6in. high, 6ft. wide. £300-350

A 19th C. pitch pine threefold screen, with three small opening panels, 6ft. high, 5ft. long fully opened. £500-600

A painted pine Bishop Saint, wearing a white and red cape, 4ft. 8in. high. £700-800 *BEL*

A pine apprentice's chest, 8 by 6 by 9 in. £40-50 *Bed*

A 19th C. pine cello case, 49in. high, 18in. wide, 12in. deep. £110-130 *WH*

A late 19th C. pine articulated artist's model, 45in. (115cm.) on an iron stand, 57in. (145cm.) overall. £1,250-1,400 *Sc*

A pine miniature wardrobe, a traveller's sample, 18 by 13 by 6 in., c.1920 £40-50 *Bed*

A 19th C. Continental pine firescreen, ornately carved, with glazed tapestry panel, 4ft. £250-300

Kitchenalia

The term Kitchenalia is one that is properly applied only to the things of the kitchen; that is, utensils for the preparation and cooking of food. Nowadays, there is a tendency for kitchens to be used for far more than just cooking and, in consequence, there is a fresh emphasis on decoration. Not only are the old tools and implements being dusted off, polished up and hung on walls, but old storage jars and tins are found to have a charm greater than that of last week's coffee jars. Many useful tools, such as carving knives, are not only less expensive, but often of better steel than their modern counterparts.

Although some of the pieces included in this section cost considerable amounts of money, the majority are in the under £50 price bracket. Indeed, many kitchenalia collectables such as biscuit tins, say, or storage jars, or teapot stands, rarely exceed £10 and almost never pass the £25 mark.

Nowadays, many items such as these are being thrown away by zealous spring cleaners, or given to jumble sales, where they may be picked up for a few pence. Another rich source is your local auction sale specialising in household items, where 'box and contents' lots selling for a pound or two will often yield goodies worth many times their purchase price. Most of these will, of course, never be valuable antiques, but all such things are likely to remain collectable and will, in consequence, rise in value as time passes by. It is only quite recently that old irons, to name but one example, have found themselves elevated from the category of disposable scrap to that of collectability; and those who saw this potential a number of years ago will have watched the value of their collections double and redouble many times over.

For many people, it is this element of chance which adds spice to collecting; the possibility that items picked up for negligible sums will suddenly be found to be worth real money. In this context, it is worth mentioning two golden rules; always seek the best possible examples of whatever it is you are collecting – the best as regards both quality and condition; and never attempt any but the most rudimentary cleaning or restoration of anything that is old. More damage is caused, and more value destroyed, by well-intentioned 'improvement' than by neglect and wilful destruction.

A 19th C. tin coffee pot, 8 by 5in. £6-8 AL

A simple corkscrew, with four-finger grip. £8-10 PC

An early Victorian brass fan-shape skimmer. £45-55

A Victorian wall-hanging candle box, with match drawer above. £25-30

A Victorian decorated flour barrel, 7½in. high, 8in. diam. £20-24 AL

A 19th C. Scandinavian beer tankard, with naive painted figures, 8½in. high. £40-50

A blue and white striped pottery 'Currants' jar and cover, the bottom stamped 'Greens Cornish Ware', 5½in. c.1920. £8-12

BAKERY

Although the home baking of bread has enjoyed a recent vogue, it is unlikely that many households will be producing enough to warrant the use of the dough bins and proving cupboards which have survived from Victorian days.

These are now considered to be decorators' items; the dough bins used to good effect as indoor plant troughs, and the proving cupboards as sturdy storage places.

Such crudely constructed items as these are not to everyone's taste but, owing to their relative scarcity (when compared with the abundance of more formal furniture) they do now, and will continue to, command very respectable prices on the open market.

A Victorian dough bin, with panelled sides and tapering legs, 30in. high, 42in. wide, 19in. deep. £100-140 AH

A 19th C. dough bin with cover, 65in. wide, 31in. deep. £70-90

A 19th C. dough bin, 32in. wide. £25-35 WH

Four East German fruitwood Dough troughs, largest – 45 by 21in., smallest – 32 by 10½in. £20-65 each WH

Two wooden dockers, for marking bread and pastry. £10-15 each PC

A selection of 19th C. brass pastry jiggers. £10-15 each MA

Two Victorian pastry cutters, 5½in. long. £10-15 each

Two pie blocks, 5½in. diam. and 4½in. diam. £20-30 each PC

A cake decorating die. £30-40 PC

A 19th C. confectionery mould. £30-40 PC

A dough knife. £5-10 PC

A decorative roller. £20-30 PC

A pine flour bin, with rope moulding around the top, acanthus leaf moulding around base, 2ft. high, 41in. wide. £550-600 Jos

A grain bin, 22in. high. £30-50 PH

144

Six 19th C. copper moulds.
£20-30 each   PC

Five 19th C. copper moulds.
£20-30 each   PC

A bread slicer. £40-60   Bed

Biscuit cutters. £5-10 each   PC

Two 19th C. copper moulds.
£20-30 each   PC

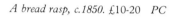

A bread rasp, c.1850. £10-20   PC

A 19th C. icing table. £40-60   PC

An early 20th C. wicker basket, 14in.
£6-7   AL

An early 20th C. wicker basket, 18in.
£7-8   AL

A 19th C. wire egg basket, 14 by 10in.
£6-8   AL

An early 20th C. wicker basket, 16in.
£6-7   AL

An early 20th C. wicker basket,
18 by 10in. £7-9   AL

An early 20th C. wicker basket, 14in.
£6-7   AL

A 19th C. Victorian picnic set, 8 by 7in.
£40-45   AL

An early 20th C. Nestle's pine wood
packing case, 18 by 13 by 6½in.
£10-12   AL

A 19th C. pine shoe cleaning box, 12 by
7½in. £11-13   AL

A 19th C. pine York County Hospital
money box, 9 by 9in. £9-11   AL

A late 19th C. solid pine till box. £10-15

A 19th C. tin black and red painted
housemaid's box, 12 by 10in.
£18-20   AL

A Victorian pine housemaid's box, with a
compartmented lift-out tray, 14in. long.
£30-35

A 19th C. pine wall-banging salt box,
with hinged lid and shaped back plate.
£25-30

A pine box. £15-20   Bed

A Victorian pine nail box, divided into
various sized compartments, 18in. long.
£10-15

A pine and fruitwood oval fronted salt
box. £35-40

A 20th C. pine shoe box, 31in. high, 20in.
wide, 16in. deep. £60-70

DAIRY

Before the days of containerised transport, factory production and supermarkets, the dairy industry was quite different from that which we know today. Many households in country districts catered largely for their own needs, and dairy smallholders would sell milk, butter and sometimes cheese to the folk living nearby.

Milk was not delivered in bottles, but collected in lidded cans. Butter was made in hand-operated churns, some holding several gallons of cream at a time; others, for household use, taking only a couple of pints.

Many old dairy implements remain. Some, such as the intaglio-carved butter moulds and prints, can still be used to serve their original purposes. Others, the butter churns, cheese strainers, skimmers and dairy bowls make interesting decorative items, and often serve other uses than those for which they were originally made.

A Victorian elm butter churn, 16½in. diam., c.1870. £65-75   SAL

Two 19th C. Welsh sycamore butter prints. £40-50   Co

A pair of Victorian boxwood butter pats, 11in. long. £12-15

Two 19th C. sycamore swan butter moulds, 4 by 3in. £30-35   SAL

A 19th C. pine butter churn, with butter pats. £35-40

A 19th C. pine curd strainer. £15-20   PF

A 17th C. Finnish butter box, with wooden nails, the seams joined with woven bark, 6in. long. £60-70

A curd cutting knife, with pine handle, c.1850. £20-25

*A selection of 19th C. butter moulds:
(r.) Ears of wheat, 2in. long, 1¾in. diam. £15-20
(c.) Strawberry plant, 3½in. long, 2½in. diam. £25-30
(l.) Rose plant, 2¼in. long, 1½in. diam. £15-20*

147

A 19th C. oak and pine iron bound cheese mould, 17in. diam. £20-25

A 19th C. Danish cheese mould, made in removable sections to release cheese, 13in. long. £30-40

A 19th C. oak and pine iron bound cheese mould, 17in. diam. £20-25

An oak and iron bound pump action butter churn, c.1880. £200-250   CGC/FRM

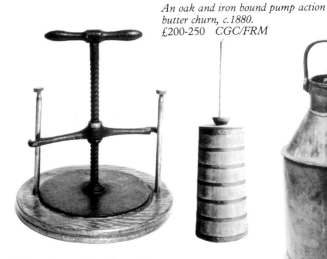

A Victorian metal and brass cheese press, on wooden base, 10in. long. £16-20   AL

A 19th C. tin milk can, 18½in. high. £11-13   AL

A 19th C. butter churn on stand, end over end, made by Lister & Co. Darsley, Yorks, 12 gallon capacity, 4ft. high. £80-90   PF

A pine cottage cheese maker. £80-90   Bed

A pine egg rack. £20-30   Bed

LAUNDRY

Although most people express from time to time a yearning for the good old days, few of us would actually appreciate the tools and working methods – particularly when it comes to the laundry.

Steam, heat and back-breaking work were very much the order of the day pretty much until the 1950's, when the washing machine industry began to come into its own.

Apart from the irons and iron stands, few of the items in this section will find homes outside the showrooms of specialist collectors – though some early washing machines are sometimes converted into standing lamps!

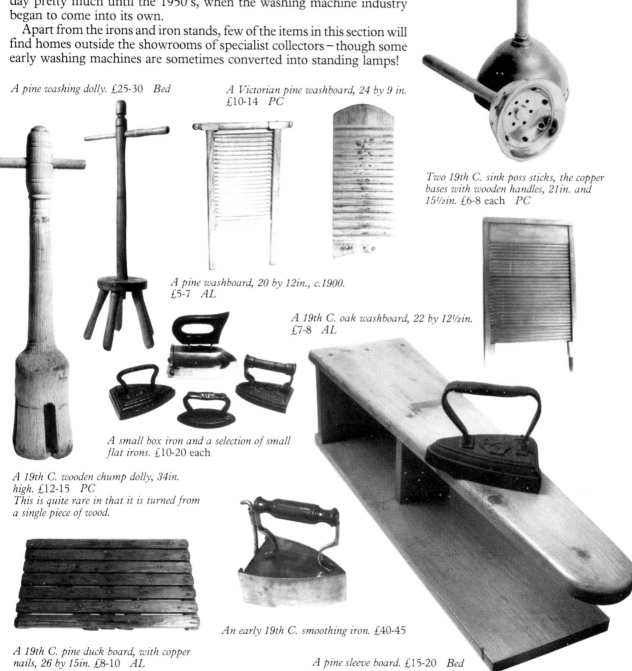

A pine washing dolly. £25-30   *Bed*

A Victorian pine washboard, 24 by 9 in. £10-14   *PC*

Two 19th C. sink poss sticks, the copper bases with wooden handles, 21in. and 15½in. £6-8 each   *PC*

A pine washboard, 20 by 12in., c.1900. £5-7   *AL*

A 19th C. oak washboard, 22 by 12½in. £7-8   *AL*

A small box iron and a selection of small flat irons. £10-20 each

A 19th C. wooden chump dolly, 34in. high. £12-15   *PC*
This is quite rare in that it is turned from a single piece of wood.

An early 19th C. smoothing iron. £40-45

A 19th C. pine duck board, with copper nails, 26 by 15in. £8-10   *AL*

A pine sleeve board. £15-20   *Bed*

149

COPPER AND BRASS

As regards dating your copper and brass – and this applies generally – few objects made of these materials bear makers' or other marks until well into the last century, when the Companies Act of 1862 caused manufacturers to mark goods with their name and trade mark. So anything that bears the words 'trade mark' or 'Limited' or 'Ltd.' may be assumed to date from no earlier than 1862.

In 1891, manufacturers were obliged to state the country of origin of export goods – and the common practice was to stamp simply 'England' on such pieces. 'Made in England' usually suggests twentieth century manufacture. But the object itself will often provide many clues...

It is only relatively recently that copper and brass kettles, for example, have acquired 'collectable' status, and in normal use they were treated with no more care than other kitchen utensils; so older examples will normally be pretty well battle-scarred. Subsequent polishing, of course, will have softened and mellowed the ravages of use, but it is unlikely that any but a modern reproduction will be completely free of dents and scratches.

Soldered seams, although sometimes used earlier, generally suggest twentieth century manufacture, as does any roughness on cast handles – earlier craftsmen always finished off their products, even on the parts that don't normally show.

A selection of 18th and 19th C. brass and iron nutcrackers. £10-25 each

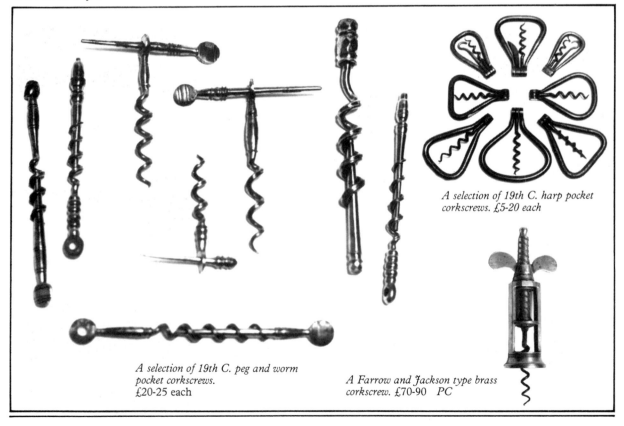

A selection of 19th C. harp pocket corkscrews. £5-20 each

A selection of 19th C. peg and worm pocket corkscrews. £20-25 each

A Farrow and Jackson type brass corkscrew. £70-90 PC

150

A selection of late 19th C. French plated iron corkscrews. £30-80 each

(t.) A Lund patent London rack corkscrew, with bottle grasp, 9½in. long, c.1860. £150-200
(b.) A Lund patent London rack corkscrew, 7½in. long, c.1860. £30-40

A 19th C. four pillar King screw. £100-150

A German spring barrel type corkscrew, c.1900. £30-35   PC

A German threaded shank type corkscrew, c.1900. £35-45   PC

A Victorian knife sharpener, 7in. long. £15-20

Two 19th C. sardine tin openers. £15-20 each

A pair of Victorian curling tongs, fitted with wooden handles, 11½in. long. £8-12

A Victorian metal strainer, with a wooden handle, 10½in. long. £4-7

A selection of 19th C. steel wick trimmers and candle snuffers. £20-50 each

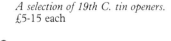

A selection of 19th C. tin openers. £5-15 each

An early 20th C. cap lifter and can opener, 10in. £10-15

An early 19th C. brass candle snuffers, with tray. £35-40   RB

A selection of keys:
(1) 18th C. steel £20-25
(2) Roman 1st C. bronze £85-105
(3) Early 19th C. steel £8-12
(4) Early 19th C. steel £8-12
(5) Early 19th C. steel £8-10 RB

A selection of 18th and early 19th C. iron and steel keys. £15-50 each

Four 19th C. brass padlocks. £15-20

An early 20th C. brass and iron fireguard, 19 by 19in. £30-35 AL

Three 19th C. iron and brass padlocks. £15-50 each

Three 19th C. brass combination locks. £15-50 each

A pair of 19th C. brass and iron fire dogs, 6 by 7in. £18-20 AL

A brass companion set, comprising: a poker, brush, tongs and shovel, on two matching stands, 23in. high, c.1900. £80-120

A brass coal scuttle, with fitted scoop and with wooden handles, 21in. high, c.1870. £200-250

A bell-metal coal scuttle, with turned wood handles and with a fitting for a scoop, 19½in., c.1800. £90-120

A Victorian brass fender, 55in. long, c.1840. £200-250

A brass and cast iron kettle stand, 8in. diam., c.1800. £60-80

A pair of brass iron trivets, 9½in. long, c.1850. £45-65

An early 19th C. brass footman. £175-225   Co

A Victorian enamelled saucepan, with fitting steel steamer, marked 'Judge Brand', 11in. high. £7-12

A brass footman, on cabriole legs, 11½in. high, c.1890-1900. £145-180

A 19th C. iron kettle, 13 by 12in. £25-30   AL

Three 19th C. brass and wood hand school or fire bells, 9in. and 12in. high. £25-45 each.

Two Victorian brass sovereign scales. £20-30 each

A brass chestnut roaster, 24½in., c.1900. £140-160

A late 19th C. brass egg cruet, with four cups, 8in. wide. £30-40

A brass candle box, 15½in. long, c.1880. £120-140

A pair of early 18th C. bell-metal candlesticks, 5½in. high. £185-200   RB

A brass jardiniere, impressed with a relief portrait, with lion mask handles, 11in. high, c.1880. £80-100

A 19th C. brass kettle on stand, 13 by 9½in. £60-65   AL

A copper kettle, 13in. high, c.1890 £80-120

A copper jelly mould, marked with 'A' beneath a crown, 3½in. high, c.1870. £60-70

A copper and tin mould. £35-45

A Victorian copper jelly mould, 3½in. high. £60-70

A pair of Victorian copper egg coddling jars, by James Bros. Down St., 3½in. high. £40-50

A 19th/20th C. metal Easter egg mould, 6in. long. £4-6

A Victorian double walled copper toddy urn, 10in. high. £50-70

A copper frying pan, 9in. diam. c.1850. £40-60

Two aluminium jelly moulds, with stands, one of a swan, the other of a rabbit, 8in. long. £5-10 each

Two late 19th C. pestle and mortars.
£18-20 each   AL

A selection of late 19th C. wood and wire
garden sieves, 14 to 22in. £8-10 each   AL

A 19th C. Kenrick brass and iron coffee
mill, 6 by 6in. £36-38   AL

An early 20th C. tin and pine Bee
Smoker, 11 by 6in. £4-5   AL

An early 20th C. brass blow lamp,
6 by 12in. £11-13   AL

A pair of Victorian tin flour dredgers,
4½in. and 3½in. £5-10 each

An early 20th C. tin watering can,
15 by 18in. £7-8   AL

Two early 20th C. plated brass ice cream
scoops. £8-9 each   AL

A Bryant & May spice tin, with graters,
5 by 5in. £20-25

A late 19th C. red and white enamelled
iron mincer, 12in. £5-6   AL

Two early 20th C. tin cheese graters, 8in.
£2-3 each   AL

A pair of Victorian sugar nips, 13in. long.
£30-35

STORAGE, WEIGHING AND MEASURING

Although we tend to think of the Victorian household as a place in which large quantities of food were consumed (Mrs. Beaton's famous 'take one dozen eggs…'), it comes as something of a surprise to find that there is generally little or no difference in size between the storage jars, tins and cupboards of the nineteenth century and those we buy new today.

Weights and scales, too, measure the same maximum quantities, give or take a little, and the only major difference between the storage capacity of the modern household and that of the nineteenth century of equivalent size, is to be found in the area of long-term storage, as made possible by the freezer cabinet.

A mid 19th C. brown and cream crock, 10in. £10-11   AL

A 19th C. dark brown and cream bread crock, 10 by 10in. £27-30   AL

A 19th C. brown and cream pottery casserole, 8 by 3in. £5-6   AL

Two stoneware wine or beer jars:

(l.) A dark bottle, with pie-crust label, marked C. Bunting, Uttoxeter, c.1820. Perfect £15-20
(r.) A bottle, marked Frank Flint, Longton, c.1880. Chipped £5-10   SW

A mid 19th C. brown and pale green crock, 11in. £10-11   AL

A 19th C. brown pottery drainer. £16-17   AL

A Brickclay jug and storage jar, both with slip or lead glaze, both perfect, c.1740. Jug £40-50.
Jar £25-30 SW

A 'Zerocool' butter cooler, in terracotta with a pottery base, 11 by 4in., c.1920.
£8-10   AL

An early Spode butter dish.
£35-40   AL

A Victorian terracotta cheese cover, 6¼in. high. £5-7   AL

A set of five matching egg cups in various colours, with gilt line rims, 2½in. high, c.1930's. £8-12

A Victorian pottery feeder, the plain white body outlined with gilt, 5in. diam. £3-8

A pottery rolling pin, with a wooden handle, marked 'Nutbrown', 'Made in England', 17in. long. £7-10

A Victorian egg beater, comprising a pottery container and metal beater, marked 'The Gourmet Egg Beater No. 5', 9in. high. £10-12

(l.) A Brickclay water holder, with manganese glaze, c. 1840.
Perfect £25-35
(c.) A Brickclay water holder, with slip and lead glaze, made at Ipstone, Staffordshire, c.1720. Perfect £50-70
(r.) A Brickclay water holder, with slip and lead glaze, c.1780. Damaged £35-40   SW

A pottery teapot stand, decorated with currants. £5-8

A Victorian shaped pottery teapot stand, moulded and decorated with roses, 7in. long. £5-8

A stoneware jar, with moulded decoration, 6in. high. £12-15

A Victorian earthenware storage jar, the brown glazed body with a band of incised decoration, 6in. high. £2-5

A blue and white striped 'Sauce' bottle, marked 'Greens Cornish Ware', 7½in. £8-10

A Victorian pottery bread plate, the rim moulded with 'Give us our daily bread' and ears of wheat, highlighted with gilt, 12in. £16-20   AL

A 'Gourmet' pie cup, glaze cracked, 3in. £10-12

A Victorian stoneware bowl, 6in. diam. £10-15

A Victorian stoneware casserole dish and cover, marked 'Lovatt's Langleyware', 7½in. diam. £10-15

A 'Gourmet' pie cup, 3in. £6-8

A Wedgwood dry body game dish, 7½in. long. £85-95

A glazed basket weave game dish, 8½in. long. £85-95

A Royal Doulton sponge dish, painted with flowers on a cream ground, the underside with factory mark and numbered D5534, 8in. diam. £6-10

Two 19th C. brown pottery jelly moulds, 4in. £10-15 each   AL

A late 19th C. Brown and Polson's blancmange mould, 5in. £22-26   AL

A 19th C. two-handled pottery jug, 8½in. £11-12   AL

A pottery sponge dish, painted with birds and bamboo, 7½in. diam. £5-10

A late 19th C. glazed multi-brown jug, chipped, 12in. high. £7-8   AL

A late 19th C. white pottery jug. £6-7   AL

A mid 19th C. brown transfer printed pottery jug, 8in. £11-13   AL

Two early 20th C. pottery jugs, 8in. high. £7-8 each   AL

Various 20th C. ice jugs. £6-7 each   AL

WEIGHING MACHINES

As soon as early man began to trade he found it necessary to invent the means of weighing things – and since that time weights and scales of many kinds and standards have been devised – some massive and crude, others small and delicate; most being attractive and, therefore, interesting to collect.

Most weights will be found to be made of iron or brass, though stone weights are not unknown, particularly in the heavier ranges, and pottery weights are to be found – and are much sought after in good condition. Use of these was made illegal in 1907 on account of their tendency to chip and grow lighter as a result. Shapes range from flat to bell in the avoirdupois range, while the metric and troy apothecaries' and pharmacists' weights are usually cylindrical. Household weights are normally more crudely made than those for commercial use, and generally lack the 'adjusting hole' in the base, into which lead was poured to bring the weight up to the standard. Any weight impressed with a six pointed star has been tested and found unsuitable for further use.

Weights, of course, would be of little use without scales. Until the introduction of spring balances in the mid-nineteenth century, all scales used the fulcrum principle which is most clearly seen in the apothecaries' scales. These have a central brass pillar on which is balanced a horizontal beam from whose ends are suspended glass or brass pans. Larger models are mounted on wooden bases which may have drawers to contain the weights, but there were many interesting pocket models made, usually in shagreen or polished wood boxes, mainly dating from the early eighteenth century.

Always useful and attractive are old grocers' and butchers' scales. These vary in value a great deal according to their state of preservation and the quantity and quality of their decorative features. Original weights of good shape also contribute significantly. Collectors particularly like the type which has a ceramic slab – often with an ornate crest and makers' name under the glaze.

A pair of early Victorian steel and brass banker's scales, 16in. high. £110-150

A pair of old platform scales, by W & T. Avery, the tray of white porcelain, together with brass weights. £180-220 BHW

A brass and cast iron set of scales, 9½in. long, c.1900. £50-60

A cast iron and copper balance, 17in. high. £65-75

TREEN

The term 'Treen' is used to describe any small wooden object associated with domestic, professional, trade or agricultural life and is a word not usually associated with any object larger than a spinning wheel. More usually treen objects are lathe-turned and are not those made by the cabinet-maker or joiner.

Decoration may take a number of forms, carving, poker-work, inlay and, in the case of some Scandinavian objects, painting.

For the beginner, treen collecting offers a reasonably inexpensive subject with many areas to choose from in which to specialise. At the lower end of the market, sewing and needlework-related items as well as Tunbridgeware and Souvenirware are worth following. Specialist dealers in treen do exist but they will normally stock only the rare and expensive: general antique shops can often prove a good hunting ground for treen. Specialised auctions sales devoted to treen rarely take place but furniture sales may have a few pieces tucked away and the house sale will always have the odd cardboard box of bits that should be inspected.

A George V wooden gallon measure, with duty mark, woodworm in base, 5in. high, 9½in. diam. £25-30

A selection of Victorian measures, one gallon, ½ gallon and peck, 7½in. the largest. £12-15 each   AL

An 18th C. hand carved wooden serving dish, 18in. diam. £85-100

An 18th C. Spanish bowl, 18in. long, 12in. wide. £70-100

Three early 20th C. elm grain measures. £15-16 each   AL

An early 19th C. sycamore bowl, 18½in. £90-120   AL

An 18th C. sycamore dairy bowl, hand turned on pole lathe, 12in. diam. £45-65

Three 19th C. lignum vitae string boxes. £30-40 each.

An unusual tree chamberstick, with snuffer stands and copper handle, 5in. high, c.1800. £235-255   HD

A pair of early 19th C. treen pots. £55-65 pair   RB

A lignum vitae string barrel, 3½in. high, c.1810. £95-125   HD

An early 19th C. Scandinavian tankard, 6in. high. £155-220 RB

A treen goblet, 5in. high. £25-30 AL

A 19th C. wooden barrel, with wicker binding and brass padlock, 8in. long. £50-60

A pair of 19th C. Continental wooden brass bound beer tankards, 6in. high. £100-120 the pair

A long handled wooden strainer, 17in. long, c.1800. £60-70

A penwork letter rack, 8in. high, c.1810. £100-120 HD

A Victorian treen pepper mill, 3in. high. £15-20

A penwork sewing box, with a picture of Brighton Pavilion, 8in. long, c.1820. £220-250

A Victorian dolls washing set, made of wood, consisting of washing bath, tub and board, the bath 6in. long. £30-35 AL

A 19th C. hatter's straw press, 19in. long. £30-35

A Victorian flour barrel, with original decorations, lined with red silk as a workbox, 9in. high, 9in. diam., c.1870. £35-40 AL

MISCELLANEOUS

A lemon reamer. £20-30   PC

A 19th C pine apple tray, 39 by 19in.
£12-15   AL

An elm toffee cutter, 24 by 12in., c.1920.
£6-8   AL

A 19th C. pine and glass egg timer,
7 by 6in. £7-8   AL

A 19th C. elm bellows, 15½in.
£30-35   AL

A pair of fine Regency penwork bellows,
14in. long. £80-100   HD

A selection of late 19th C. deeply carved
bread boards, from 11in. to 14in.
£10-20 each   AL

A 19th C. lacquer decorated bellows,
12½in. £40-45   AL

A late 19th C. green glass bottle, 18in.
£9-10   AL

A 19th C. pine plate rack, 2ft. 6in. high.
£40-45

A 19th C. pine plate rack, with shaped
sides. £45-50

A rare 19th C. Alexandra Inhaler, with
multicolour decoration, glass tube missing,
5in. £19-20   AL

Three late 19th C. pottery Virol jars, 5in.
£5-6 each   AL

Three late 19th C. wooden nutcrackers,
German or Austrian. £50-60 each

An early 20th C. brown and dark cream glazed jug and basin, 17in. diam. £35-40   *AL*

A treen string holder, 5in. high. £65-75

A late 19th C. white pottery shaving mug, 4in. £7-8   *AL*

A peg wooden doll, 11in. high, c.1920. £25-50   *AL*

A 19th C. wire and mahogany birdcage, 16 by 14in. £35-40   *AL*

An early 20th C. Sussex trug, 21 by 14in. £18-20   *AL*

A 19th C. pine barrel, 6½ by 7in. £18-21   *AL*

A late 19th C. wood and wire toasting fork, 16in. £4-5   *AL*

An 18th C. copper ladle, 15in. long. £18-19   *AL*

A Danish stove, 187cm. high. £700-800   *BEL*

A set of 19th C. folding oak book-ends, 13 by 5in. £9-11   *AL*

A 19th C. pine letter rack, 14 by 9in. £11-13   *AL*

A rare Welsh sycamore love spoon. £350-400   *Co*

A Norwegian stove, 182cm. high, c.1880. £850-950   *BEL*

Reproduction Pine Furniture

The reproduction pine industry has seen an unprecedented boom over the last few years. With antiques becoming more difficult to find and prices fluctuating from one sale to the next, many people have turned to reproduction furnitures as a more stable, certain purchase.

With a reproduction you know exactly what you are buying. You may miss the excitement of the chase – the chance of picking up an undiscovered bargain – but at least you know in advance the piece will fit and precisely how much you have to pay for it.

We must also remember that not everyone wants to possess old, 'second hand' furniture. Some people like the old style but would prefer a brand new piece. This is catered for by the ever expanding reproduction industry. It is also often commercial sense to construct from new rather than getting involved in the expensive business of restoration. This is particularly true for pine.

One argument used against buying reproduction furniture is that it doesn't stand the investment test. An antique, at the very least, keeps up with inflation and has often been proved to be an excellent investment. New furniture, on the other hand, depreciates considerably the minute it's purchased. However manufacturers of reproductions (or tomorrow's antiques!) have been proved right by the number of reproductions from the early and mid twentieth century which are now appearing in auctions and realising prices considerably above their estimates.

To buy or not to buy an antique or a reproduction? It's very much a question of taste, but it is fair to say it would be a mistake to ignore this very buoyant area of the pine furniture market.

A reproduction pine bureau.
£137 YP

A reproduction pine dressing table.
£83 YP

A reproduction pine linen press.
£118 YP

A reproduction pine bookcase.
£95 YP

A reproduction pine pedestal desk.
£153 YP

Index to Advertisers

Pine Stripping Specialists

Allens Antiques,
Moor Farm, Stapleford, Lincs.
Tel: (052 285) 392

Antique Pine,
The Rookery, Salter Hebble,
Halifax, West Yorkshire.
Tel: (0422) 45445

Antique Pine,
Yorkshire Stripping Service,
Mill Farm, Kirk Hammerton, Yorks.
Tel: (0901) 30451

Drawers,
45 Plymouth Road, Buckfastleigh, Devon.
Tel: (0364) 42848

Enloc Antiques,
Old Corporation Yard,
Knotts Lane, Colne, Lancs.
Tel: (0282) 861417

Fine Pine of Harbertonford,
Zeaston Farm, South Brent, Devon.
Tel: (036 47) 2502

Garry Blanch,
Mounts Farm, Benenden, Cranbrook, Kent.
Tel: (0580) 240622

Graham Porter,
31 Whitehorse Street, Baldock, Herts.
Tel: (0462) 895351

In-Situ Paint Stripping Co.,
134 Lots Road, London, S.W.10
Tel: 01.351 4333

Knightsbridge Antiques,
43c Chipstead Valley Road,
Coulsdon, Surrey.
Tel: 01.668 0148

Kwik Strip (U.K.) Limited,
Units 1/2, The 306 Estate,
242 Broomhill Road, Brislington, Bristol.
Tel: (0272) 772470

With branches at:

Bath, Avon.
Tel: (0225) 315541

Bexhill-on-Sea, Sussex.
Tel: (0424) 223090

Edinburgh, Scotland.
Tel: (031 652) 1645

Glasgow, Scotland.
Tel: (041 778) 4043

Gloucester.
Tel: (0452) 26726

Hull, Humberside.
Tel: (0482) 28966

Liverpool, Merseyside.
Tel: (051 521) 8500

Rochester, Kent.
Tel: (0634) 41212

Shrewsbury, Salop.
Tel: (0743) 246359

Southampton, Hants.
Tel: (0703) 332605

Tipton, West Midlands.
Tel: (021 520) 6705

Langley Antiques,
15 High Street, Kings Langley, Herts.
Tel: (092 77) 64417

Romic,
4 Evron Place, Hertford, Herts.
Tel: (0992) 552880

Scallywag,
The Old Church, Wren Road,
Camberwell Green, London, S.E.5
Tel: 01.701 5353

Scar Top Antiques,
Far Scar Top, Stanbury,
Nr. Keighley, W. Yorks.
Tel: (0535) 42585

Stone-Wares. The Stripped Pine Shop,
24 Radford Street, Stone, Staffs.
Tel: (0785) 81500

Strip-It,
Lady B. Marina, Portslade, Sussex.
Tel: (0273) 597200

Tealby Pine,
Goltho Hall, Goltho, Wragby,
Nr. Lincoln, Lincs.
Tel: (0673) 858789

The Craftsman,
16 Bridge Street, Hungerford, Berks.
Tel: (0488) 82262

The Pine Cone,
15 Gwydir Street, Cambridge.
Tel: (0223) 311203

The Pine Mine,
96-100 Wandsworth Bridge Road,
London, S.W.6
Tel: 01-736 1092

Yesterday's Pine,
13 Dunstable Street, Ampthill, Beds.
Tel: (0525) 402260

Pine Restorer Specialists

Graham Porter,
31 Whitehorse Street, Baldock, Herts.
Tel: (0462) 895351

Period Pine Restoration,
Green Lane Farm, Bethersden, Kent.
Tel: (023 382) 382

Yesterday's Pine,
13 Dunstable Street, Ampthill, Beds.
Tel: (0525) 402260

PINE INDEX